D1098331

GAMBLING WITH FAILURE

ANTONIO D'ALFONSO

GAMBLING WITH FAILURE

TORONTO

Exile Editions
2006

The original edition was published in Canada in 2005.
This second edition, containing major revisions, was published
by Exile Editions Ltd.
20 Dale Avenue
Toronto, Ontario, M4W 1K4
Telephone: 416 485 9468
www.ExileEditions.com

Copyright © 2005, 2006 by Antonio D'Alfonso
The use of any part of this publication, reproduced, transmitted
in any form or by any means, electronic, mechanical,
photocopying, recording or otherwise stored in a retrieval
system, without the expressed written consent of the publisher, is
an infringement of the copyright law.

Library and Archives Canada Cataloguing in Publication
D'Alfonso, Antonio
Gambling with failure : essays / Antonio D'Alfonso.
ISBN 1-55096-656-1
I. Title.
PS8557.A456G35 2005   C813'.54   C2005-906705-5

Second printing.
Design and Composition: ADA
Cover Painting: Gabriela Campos
Printed in Canada: Imprimerie Gauvin

The publisher would like to acknowledge the financial
assistance of The Canada Council for the Arts.

Canada Council   Conseil des Arts
for the Arts   du Canada

Contents

To Barry Callaghan
and Elana Wolff

Dans le secret de mon cœur, je ne me sens d'humilité que devant les vies les plus pauvres ou les grandes aventures de l'esprit. Entre les deux se trouve aujourd'hui une société qui fait rire.

Albert Camus,
L'envers et l'endroit

She knows there's no success like failure
And that failure is no success at all.

Bob Dylan,
"Loves Minus Zero/No Limit"

By Way of Introduction

Wish I could write like a scholar. I can't. Being the result of a crazy *mélange* of cultures, I am too fragmented to think in a linear fashion. There are no footnotes at the bottom of the page, the bibliography, if any, is modest, uneven, eclectic. There are too many repetitions in what I write, even though I treat each repetition like a musical leitmotif: a melody that is ever so slightly altered, modified, inverted, enhanced by the context. Much like a *bolero*.

I wanted to be a great person but I have come to realize that I have not achieved what I set out to do. Dreams are valid as dreams. Once you try to touch the dream, like you would an apple, it becomes an object, and the moment you fall onto the world of real objects you find yourself climbing back to square one; that is, dreaming.

It is because I am a dreamer that I have never become a scholar. I write this not to undermine the scholar's work; I respect scholars and owe a great deal to the men and women who have taken the work that I have done seriously, both as writer and as editor. I simply don't have a passion for scholarly methodolgy. Writing is a tool that complements the other tools I have at my disposal.

I started to write because I wanted to touch another person by the means that I believed, at the time, to be the least harmful and the least intrusive.

Writing is anything but harmless or distant. Our world runs on the *malentendu*, as Baudelaire said. *Malentendu* does not simply mean misunderstanding; it can, but it does not have to.

What occurs is more like finding a fault in the found object, having a fault in the understanding. You understand what is being said to you, but you are pushing the understanding in a slightly different direction than the one intended. One might say that this is precisely what "misunderstanding" means in normal North American English usage. But to misunderstand puts the weight of the fault on one pole of the equation: the receiver. What happens if the fault in the understanding occurs at the other pole, on the sender's side, not the receiver's? How can I be so sure that what I am saying is correct, true, valuable? What if what I am saying is the product of sheer vanity? My head might have been struck by a baseball bat, and what I am uttering may be gibberish.

There is one barometer to understanding: oneself. I have only myself to compare myself to. Not that I am the one best equipped to properly understanding; I may very well be the worst person to compare myself to. And yet I must rely on myself as a gauge of understanding, or on whatever it is that makes me the one I am. I am so conditioned by the world I live in that I doubt much of what I am saying can be of use to anyone, myself included. I mirror what I have seen.

I begin to dream when I write. I speak the dream that I am dreaming. I try to describe how the dreaming comes to be within me, but also how to interpret this dream of mine. I want to make sure that there is the least misunderstanding possible.

I aim at an understanding with as few faults in texture as possible. I stumble, I roll over, I jump back up on my feet, and off I walk into another room where a bunch of men and women are standing and exchanging the contents of their separate and common dreams.

I love to listen to people's dreams; I love to listen to people tell me their dreams. I usually have no clue what these dreams mean; I am not even sure I can fully grasp why this person is telling his or her dreams, but I try very hard to see what it is that is out there, in front of me, while doing the exact same thing that I am doing.

It is in my best of interests to listen to others: friends and enemies. Keep your friends close by, but keep your enemies closer still.

I do not wish to imply that every person I meet is a potential enemy; that would be paranoia. What I mean is that one does not meet many friends in life. You have to make do with yourself in the company of strangers. To be the very best of yourself, try to be loving, caring, generous, and at the same time know that all of this intensity might last only that one instant, and that the moment might never arise again.

Human contact has become such a financial commodity that it is very difficult to share a decent glass of wine with someone before he or she rushes off round the corner and escapes the clutches of friendship.

When I started publishing my own writings I became aware of the ways I could divulge myself in public. I did not want writing to be construed as an excuse for vanity, arrogance, or exhibitionism. Because I have elaborated a style which is based on my person as a social model for the world we live in, it soon became imperative for me to cut off the excess fat that self-exposure initially brings out.

I crave to compose a simple sentence that expresses one idea at a time. Though very much a desire, I cannot describe my family life; I prefer exposing the gray matter at work. I do not take myself for a good writer, but I walk on a road that has not been walked on. I am not sure what I say is right. I do not even know if my ideas can ever be transformed into something real. What counts for me is to describe what I see around me.

I never for a single second expected my writings would bring about the sort of animosity that *In Italics,* its French version *En Italiques,* and *Duologue: On Culture and Identity* (written with Pasquale Verdicchio) did. The silence surrounding these three books is telling of the sort of literary world we live in. I have read some fairly negative comments about my work, and I have had to admit that those reviewers touched on defects that needed to be corrected. Writing entails rewriting the same book until we get it right.

I have to be careful of abstraction, I have to learn to be a smoother writer, less fragmented, more linear in my style. I try hard not be abstract. In many ways it all seems beyond my control because in the end I write the way I speak, and I speak all languages badly. Improper syntax doesn't help for proper understanding. Or does it? Lack of linguistic skill trips me up. I am very bad when it comes to idiomatic expressions. Instead of saying "I put my foot in my mouth," I will turn the words around and unwittingly mumble, "I put my mouth on my foot."

A dyslexic mistake turns out to be a good joke, but has it conveyed what I had initially intended? There is no room for this sort of humor in boardroom decorum. Not that humor is not tolerated; it is, especially when spiced up with all type of uncivil innuendoes. Yet we do not like to have someone hanging around us who asks questions nonstop. "Let's get to the point," they smile.

All I want is to walk up that yellow-brick road of modern identity and see if it will lessen the hatred that nations have injected us with. People call it *patriotism*. I do not know what to call it. I love people and care little for the nation-state.

By the late 1980s, I could feel in my bones that the Italian culture was dying away. By this I do not mean to say that Italian was dead as *my* culture. That sort of loss is of interest to no one. What I felt as a child is what UNESCO and Jean Paul II declared a few years ago: Italian culture is on its way to extinction. There are not enough people in the world to keep the Italian culture alive. Work for the survival of this culture should have been undertaken a hundred years ago. It wasn't.

Some men and women preferred to take the path to nationhood, instead of trying to bridge the Italic communities around the world, Italy included. The Italian experience in a federal republic failed. Fascism was a sick attempt at trying to solve the problem. You cannot solve a problem with a problem. The Italian nation has extended the right to vote to Italian emigrants. I wonder what such a proposal intends to accomplish.

A comment like "We are all Italians" is just another cunning attempt at dumping the bins of distrust onto the Other.

Past horrors can be detected in the term *we.*

There never was an Italian *we.* The Italian is a conservative individualist, the Italian progressive included. Compared to a gathering of Quebecois or French intellectuals, Italian intellectuals are a strangely conservative lot. I had to fetch radical ideals elsewhere.

Critics have reproached me for being a francophile. "You write like a French person." Yet I discovered French culture at the same time as I was discovering Italian culture. I have invested a lot of time and energy in trying to understand what Italian culture is; it has become my business to explain it. I am not sure that my work has yielded any palpable results. Italians are no better off now than they were in the beginning of the century.

The problems Italians face as a community are many, and nothing fruitful will come about until Italians sit down and organize. I am happy to have discovered that Italian philosopher, Piero Bassetti, thinks about such issues as I do. He too uses the word *Italics* in his 2002 interview, *Glocals and Locals,* with Swiss writer Sergio Roic. Of course, I was upset that he might have picked up the word in some garbage bin where someone had thrown my own *In Italics.* But I don't care. His book has made my solitary quest less solitary. I can actually say I am no longer alone.

The French culture in me blossomed gradually, often in the most unexpected ways. There is a vitality in French-speaking Quebec and French Canada that is totally lacking elsewhere in this country. I find Italian communities in Italy and abroad very set in their ancient rigid ways. When culture becomes xenophobic, its days of glory can be counted on the fingers of both hands.

Tomorrow's cultures will be acquired cultures. Learned cultures. Innocent cultures are long gone. Perhaps there never was such a thing as a pure culture. What is culture anyway? Social customs, language, food, organized religion? I have no idea. The more I read on the topic the less I know. A more meaningful question might be not "What is culture" but "What can culture become?"

Culture should not imitate itself. A fossilized culture closes its door to other cultures. Nevertheless, no culture can be transcended without suffering, nor can culture spread itself out limitlessly without risking disfiguration. There must be a third or fourth term here, somewhere, something in between what was and what must become. Discovering this other term is what interests me.

Culture should be conscious of itself and yet also be frivolous. Analyze but also laugh. Cry but also comfort. The question right now is whether or not there are people out there interested enough in a living culture. We have become such experts in cultural necrophilia: we unearth the dead with the hope of concealing what is being done at the present time.

The savage obsession in the arts for modern neo-classical remakes is quite telling of this fear of what lies on the table before us. Better to look at the past than deal with the issues at hand. We have other worries that trouble us, more urgent matters to discuss. In the end, I am not sure culture matters.

Box-office success creates dead cultures, for it fossilizes what should be palpitating with passion. Success excludes, and elimination reduces the chances of connections. If the spotlight falls on that one item, and if that one item is not strong enough to carry the expectations of the buyers, people will turn away, dissatisfied. Putting all our eggs in one basket is very dangerous.

No one truly cares about culture. And when they do, it is usually in time of war to stress the idea that "ours" is a better culture than "theirs." (The password today has become *civilization*.)

Culture is what is left over when there is no more money in the bank vaults. Capitalism teaches us to believe that to eat a real or a genetically modified tomato makes no difference.

We have grown accustomed to false bread, robots, androids. How false a thing should be is no longer relevant unless it affects our powers. You sell me shrimp and call it corn flakes. What happens to those who are allergic to crustaceans?

I am sitting on a corn flake, to quote John Lennon, feeling a little dizzy with these unresolved questions, a little depressed because looking for solutions to these problems seems futile.

That I started to write in the first place because I wanted to seduce a girl seems outright ludicrous. Yes, it was a need for love that led me to put words down on paper.

I continue to write because I have not been able to seduce the woman I love, the readers I love.

We don't like people who rock the boat.

I am kneeling in that same boat. I too am being rocked, and suddenly I feel nauseous.

Unlike Columbus, I know there is no land out there to be found. Or if there is land out there, it is not mine to have. My brother has sold what could have been mine to those guys and gals on the other side who are always ready to pay more than I can ever afford.

The Red Herring

One of my favorite devices in film is the red herring. No, not the *Clupea harengus,* the smoked herring served at parties, but that thing that someone hangs in front of your nose and diverts you for an instant from the truth. Long enough for you to smack your nose right against a brick wall. Just where you were promised an opening, a door, a few seconds before. Alfred Hitchcock was a master of red herrings. So is Roman Polanski. But the true masters are politicians, especially their flunkies. Why? Because the red herring works best in real life.

The red herring does not smell, although its fetid odor will knock you off your feet once you realize that you've been had real good. The red herring is a promise, an object of desire, that a hypnotist dangles before your eyes like a blue jewel. In the end you are left standing there, *come un bacala,* as my father would say, your mouth open wide with foolish wonder, asking yourself why is it that you did not see it coming.

You never see it coming. If you did, it would not be a red herring.

Lying with intelligence.

Two politicians scream at one another in front of the home of elderly citizens: one offers borrowed money; the other screams that the money is a scam.

Who is telling the truth?

I attended a meeting recently where I was offered the gracious experience of being taken for a fool. The meeting had to do with issues on culture and politics and politics passing itself for culture.

Someone who is (was) the president of the association of some cultural group (let's leave it unnamed) wished to pass a motion that would put a halt to membership. A strange motion, if you ask me, that left me dumbfounded.

While the person explained why the doors had to be shut, I quietly stood up, tiptoed to the entrance door of the hall we were sitting in (about 200 of us), looked outside, turned around, and naively (well, perhaps not so naively but, let's say, for the sake of argument, I pretended to be naive) interrupted the speaker:

"Why this motion? There is no line-up outside the door?"

Everybody started to laugh.

When I noticed the beads of sweet rolling down the president's temples, spin round his cheeks, and somersault onto his shirt collar, it dawned on me that I would have to answer my own question.

"This motion is a red herring. You don't want to prevent people from entering our association. What you are asking us to do is to make it impossible for the membership to throw delinquent members out of the association."

At this point the vice-president pulled the microphone from beneath the president's chin and admitted that the nail had been hit on the head. The vice-president reiterated how membership in the association was based on citizenship, and revealed that the company of one of our members who, by accident, happened to be the president, had just been purchased by a foreign firm, thus rendering his company's Canadian ownership automatically void.

"No problem," I grinned. "He will have to quit the association."

But that was the problem: if he left, the Canadian government would soon discover the truth and pull the plug on the subsidies for his company. No publishing house in Canada can survive without grants.

When people speak of culture in Canada (or for that matter anywhere), listen carefully to what is being said. Then pull back, as a film camera would, and try to see the larger picture. Catch what it is that they are really talking about. More often than not, you will discover the actual story unfolding beyond the story being told.

When people complain there is no money for the arts in Canada, it usually means that the money there simply cannot go to the artists who are appearing in the horizon, well, popping up around the corner; that is, our children.

The main problem most countries must solve in the near future is what to do with the children of working-class immigrants? It is as though they never expected that the earlier need for manpower would branch out into families and families' children. Nor that, one day, these children would find the urge to express their experiences artistically.

What to do with these artists-to-be who find

themselves crowded in front of a massive wall where hangs a sign that reads: "You are not welcome in this building?"

At a time when pluriculturalism should be flourishing in most countries, the doors of parliament are shutting down. Flunkies repeat non-stop that there is no money in the vaults of the government. Truth or lie? Or is this a smelly red herring?

Answering Questions
Interview with Susana Molinolo

Susan Molinolo: *Where were you born? Where did you grow up?*

Antonio D'Alfonso: I was born in Montreal and grew up in downtown Montreal and, after 1960, in Ville Saint-Michel, the north end (in those days) of the island of Montreal. It is a small city which was annexed by Montreal in the late 1960s. As with all mega-projects city bureaucrats invented an intelligent excuse to destroy an incredibly vibrant part of Quebec. Today 19th Avenue where we used to live looks pretty much like a war zone.

Sure, you still find tiny spots filled with memories, but dirty businesses of all kinds have turned it into a under-class neighborhood. This wasn't always the case. I like to believe that our part of town was pretty much middle class. The workers who worked there owned their houses and land. Our street was clean and crime-free. I do not recall hearing of any incidents of serious crime during the years we lived there. I heard of one hold-up, but that was a little event in a very small bank. St. Michel worked very much like a small community, even if the neighbors did not converse much with one another. Knowing that your neighbor was a hardwork-ing person sufficed to reassure pretty much everyone on the block.

I speak of 19th Avenue, between Ruskin (now

Everett) and Dickens (Villeray) as though it were the hubbub of Quebecois culture; it wasn't. At least, not in the bigger picture of things cultural, but I was fortunate enough to have met some pretty fascinating men and women who encouraged me to explore the unknown territory of culture. Perhaps this was due to the mixture of different European cultures that gathered there.

I stress European, because today no one would consider Europeans immigrants. Color, however, was never an issue. To be an immigrant meant that you came from somewhere else, somewhere that was not here. For instance, my friend's family came from French Ontario, Castlemann. That's next door, yet he acted in ways that were not common to the rest of us. His family, though Catholic, was somewhat Protestant-like in its customs.

I have known Quebecois families all my life and I must tell you there were attitudes held by people from urban Ontario that were not those of people from urban Quebec. Michel, who was born in Montreal, had to learn, like myself, how to be become a Montrealer. There were two Irish families, both Catholic, which did not speak English. The only Protestant family, which lived next door, was the only family that spoke English at home. The Irish boasted the fact that they spoke French and did not speak to the English family that didn't, though they had a French-sounding name. Somehow we all knew that the family wanted to be different.

We also had a family of gays and lesbians that lived right in front of us. This did not bother us one bit; they certainly taught me how to feel deep sympathy for their plight, which is not an easy one (though the Canadian government is doing much to rectify the flow of things anti-homosexual). We had Scots as well, but they too spoke French. We were the only Italian family on the block and we spoke an Italian dialect. Other Italian families lived further west and, later, when they created it, in Saint Leonard.

We all spoke French. My sister and I went to English school but we spoke French. Our world was French-speaking, and our cultural references, except for what was transmitted on TV, was Quebecois, not French-Canadian, since we did not know what that term meant. Being French Quebecois (a mixture of Europeans of different origins and Amerindians), we chose to speak French. Don't ask me why, it is a fact. Everyone did.

It is thanks to the French Quebecois language that I got a glimpse of what culture outside Italian could be. I say "could be" because culture, even as a young man, was some strange creature that kept on moving. Culture has to change, and all our activities were directed towards change. We started cultural groups and learned to work with one another.

Later I discovered music, and that changed my way of thinking totally. My life was turned around the day my father came back home with an archtop Commodore guitar (probably an off-shoot of Harmony). Music soon became the way for me to express myself, whether with a band or alone, as a lousy folk singer.

S.M.: *As a child, what occupations did you dream of?*

A.D.: What did I dream of? Two things: leaving

Montreal, and being an artist. I can't explain it, for the life of me, why I wanted to leave Montreal. When I took long walks alone, all I ever thought about was leaving. Not running away, for I come from a happy family; no, all I wanted to do was move to a different world. I know now what that world (Europe) is, but I did not know it then, since my parents never brought us with them on their trips to Italy. They probably thought that we would be bored or horrified to see where they had lived as children. Were they ashamed of where they came from? All I know is that they never invited us to go. They later sent my sister and me, separately, on a trip to Italy. But that was only because they wanted us to meet my mother's parents (my paternal grandparents lived with us).

Music enabled me to travel, staying put on a chair plucking my guitar and bass. Being in a band with other Italians helped me understand that we shared something in common, music of course, but also an Italian background. Unfortunately, we never used that background to any purpose, except in the meals we ate. Had we incorporated our Italian tastes to the music we were playing we might have become something. All we ever did was repeat, quite unconsciously I must add, what was being done by Italians living in the U.S.A. We played music by the Rascals, Frank Sinatra, and other crooners. A rock band trying to play popular jazz.

It was once I discovered Montrealer Leonard Cohen's first LP in the mid-1960s that music, urban music from my home town, took on a different significance. Suddenly I wanted to be more than a copier of others. I felt quite viscerally that I could do something truly fine by following this new road. Something else changed me forever and that was listening to King Crimson LPs.

From that moment on, I became aware that, if I was going to play music, or do anything for that matter, I had to study it very seriously, which I was not ready to do. I decided to quit music and applied to university (I had been earning money playing on a weekly basis with the band). I chose school and came back to music later, at the birth of my daughter (which led to my first CD, *Night Talks*).

S.M.: *Where did you study? What degrees do you have?*

A.D.: I studied at Loyola College. I wanted to go to McGill but was turned down (perhaps the first bead on a long string of bad luck). I do not regret going to Loyola and studying with Jesuits. They shaped me into the person I am today.

Situated on the west side of Montreal, I lived for the first time in my life beside people who were totally English-speaking. Where I came from we studied in English schools, but we lived in a French-speaking environment (the music we played with the band was English at first, but soon we understood that, if we were going to "make it," we had to start singing in French, and we finally did. We even changed our band's name from Togetherness to L'Unité – I don't recall it being a reference to the Communist newspaper *Unità* in Italy).

At Loyola I studied sociology and biology. It was in taking a psychology course that I discovered theatre! In those days, the late 1960s and early 1970s, the new arts were administered by the Department of Psychology. Go figure. Says much about what social scientists thought about film, photography, and television.

One afternoon, I ran into an acquaintance from John F. Kennedy, the high school we had attended, and it was he who offered me a role in his short film. I accepted, not realizing that I had stepped on the threshold of a totally new world. Film. I had seen the majestic works by Robert Bresson and Jean-Luc Godard, but I never once thought that I would actually study to be a filmmaker myself. I got my B.A. in Communication Arts (film) in 1975. I shot three short films and worked on a dozen films written and directed by friends.

In 1977, after having spent a year or so in the real working world, I decided to go back to university. I don't know exactly why, I had fallen on a book by Patrick Straram le bison ravi, *Questionnement socratique,* where he mentioned Roland Barthes. After reading Barthes' books, I told myself that I wanted to study semiology, and more specifically one film, *Mouchette,* by Robert Bresson. In those days no one had heard of semiology. And so I applied to the Université de Montréal and studied with a semiologue, the only one in Canada, who specialized in architecture.

I received my M.Sc. in semiology in 1979. Later that year, I got married and drove down to Mexico, where I decided to make a living as a writer and publisher.

S.M.: *Favorite thing to do when you need to get away from writing/editing/words?*

A.D.: I play music. I take photographs of people I meet. I love spending hours talking with people. I used to watch films, a lot of films, but I find most films today insipid.

What can I say, when one runs into giants like Robert Bresson, John Cassavetes, Roberto Rossellini, François Truffaut, Ingmar Bergman, Pier Paolo Pasolini, or Federico Fellini, contemporary films seem like larger-than-life computer games. Not only are the scripts computer fabricated, actors too appear to be computer-generated. In all honesty, I prefer spending time bathing in the warmth of nice people. One finds dedicated artists among them.

S.M.: *Tell me a bit about your family while you were growing up?*

A.D.: My sister has a different take on my family. I think we lived pretty much in a loving environment, though less when my father's parents were alive and living under the same roof as us. My grandmother and my mother were not fond of one another, but certainly after, and often, during those dark periods of intense quarreling between the female adults in the house, one could actually touch the love my parents had for one another.

My father worked three shifts to make ends meet. My grandfather had suffered a stroke which left him partially paralyzed; he could hardly speak because of the muscle impediments around his mouth. I had to find affection whenever I could and so I would devise ways to steal that affection from my mother. Being the more fragile one, my sister received all the love parents could offer.

I got my share too but I had to find ways to make sure that I would never be skipped. Maybe my need to create was, in the beginning, nothing but a cry for affection.

My mother tells me about one such cry. I remember the event one way, but I will tell it to you as my mother tells it.

The washing-machine is on. The pots on the stove are boiling with water. My sister is sound asleep; she needs something my mother doesn't have. My mother says she has to go across to the store and fetch the item. I say, "No problem." I love being alone.

She steps out, runs across the street to the corner store and, when she comes back, the door is locked. I have locked all the doors to the house, so that no one can come in, not my mother, especially not my mother. She is outside smiling at first, then she starts to beg, and finally screams in Italian, "Open the door before I kill you!"

She is beyond of herself.

Standing tall with all of my five years, I ask her to ring the doorbell. "Pretend you are a stranger."

My mother rings the doorbell.

I walk up to the door and tell her that my parents forbid me to open the door to strangers.

"Open the damn door," my mother screams.

I don't. I walk back to the washroom and pull out my father's shaving equipment: the razor with a killer blade and soap in a plate. I beat the soap to a rich lather which I apply to my face, just like my dad and, just like my dad, I start shaving. Slice. I cut my chin in two. Blood gushes out of my face. But I don't cry. I rush to my mother, now banging on the door, who almost

ANSWERING QUESTIONS

faints, and say in Italian, quite proud of myself, "Look, Mamma, I can shave like Daddy."

I finally open the door and, after my mother wraps my face with bandages, get the whacking of my life. My sister is crying, the washing-machine floods over, the pots are burned.

S.M.: *What are you working on these days?*

A.D.: Nothing much. I wrote a film script, *Consent,* with actress Jennifer Dale. We are waiting for it to be filmed this year. My novel, *Fabrizio's Passion,* was published in Italy, an ancient dream come true. I have translated the selected poems by Louise Dupré and Paul Bélanger, both fine Quebecois poets. I have started a book of essays on failure. I also spend most of my days trying to keep Guernica Editions from sinking. I am living the worst period of my life, on all accounts, and it is major work staying alive. Translating the works of other writers helps me practice my chops, without having to deal with my own hang-ups.

S.M.: *What are your criteria for selecting a manuscript?*

A.D.: I have no real criteria for choosing one manuscript over another. My choices have to do with details and these details should change my own life. I am not interested by anything that smells like "something" I have smelled already. My premise is always: "If it doesn't change me, it will do nothing for culture in general." A tough stance to uphold, but the only way to be as an editor.

I started Guernica to change the face of the Canadian literary landscape. We were the first to introduce the notion of multiculturalism in literature back in the late 1970s. We are not about to declare bankruptcy now, regardless of the criticism being thrown into our faces.

S.M.: *Why are books so important to you?*

A.D.: Books are not important at all in fact. People are. A book is something we drop in a friend's lap, with the hope that it will make him laugh or cry, even if only for one second. I used to have great expectations about literature. I no longer do. Like modern film, sameness has trivialized books. Books are not a necessity, nor a commodity. They are entirely useless. More so in English Canada than in French Canada and Quebec.

I know this is an impossible and unpopular position to maintain but I don't see how in our global context one more English-language book can possibly alter the manner in which things get done in anglophone nations more powerful than English Canada.

If you speak of language, American English has totally transformed the way one uses English, everywhere, and in England in particular. American English is a necessary tool for the advancement of English-speaking cultures. I don't see what new water Canadian English can bring to the water mill.

No wonder the most famous English-language writers are published by large American presses. They are acting as Americans. Who cares to publish with a Canadian press today? No one. Those who do, do so as an interim, before they are purchased by an American publisher. I have nothing against American publishers. I wonder what complaints they would have if all American writers were to publish, say in England, with British presses?

32

The Canadian press seems like a futile dinosaur in the book industry. If Canadian writers were to publish exclusively with Canadian presses, if they would all publish exclusively with one press, then perhaps English Canada would have something fresh to offer. But with writers being traded like paper napkins, the entire industry has become as fragile as a used paper napkin.

There are books that are important, and I would not be the person I am if there were no French-language writers working in Canada today. Perhaps all writers in Canada should be writing in French, since the French language has to be pushed off its throne the same way British English was dethroned by American English.

The Italian language needs such a jolt as well. It would be too much to ask Canadian writers to stop writing in English and French and adopt Italian as the language of their writing. But that too could be a solution to our cultural crisis. (Pluriculturalism means changing who one is.)

French-language books published in Canada are essential reading for all Canadians. Nearly one hundred percent of the writers in Quebec publish with Quebecois publishers. When I read Quebecois writers in French – reading them in English is valid only as an exercise in curiosity – I get a clearer sense of what places this country (or, at least, part of the country) is moving to. The books I love, outside those written by the people I know, are those of the past. I have no favorite writer, nor do I pay much attention to what scholars consider essential and fundamental. I take what I want from world literature: when a book changes my way of thinking about being a human, I keep it close to my heart; if it doesn't, I simply toss it aside and forget it.

S.M.: *How many languages do you speak? Read? Write? Where did you learn them?*

A.D.: I speak three languages, English, French, Italian, and I speak them all badly. I spoke Spanish, and still do, but since I had to chose between Italian and Castillano Spanish − my mind kept tripping into the pitfalls of "false friends" (similar words that have different meanings) − I am a little rusty. I read Castillano, yet prefer Catalan, for it is a language that has much to offer right now to the planet. I would like to learn Portuguese, German, and Japanese.

Not having a mother tongue I can write in − our dialect from Abruzzi e Molise is a spoken language − it is difficult for me to feel at ease in any language. Yet I am able to follow a conversation in most languages, even if the details escape me. I love languages, they are windows that open onto my neighbors' gardens. I am curious to learn how my neighbors live. They might have something that might make me a better human.

S.M.: *What would you do if you won a million dollar lottery?*

A.D.: I don't gamble in any way. I have other vices; gambling goes against the grain of my very essence. I don't understand the meaning of your question. I will never become a millionaire. I work to earn money. I have dedicated thirty years of my life to literature and books, and yet Guernica appears nowhere in the history of English-Canadian publishers. I have no money in my bank account, no old-age pension. The government reclaimed money it had given Guernica for publishing, aware that in doing so it would undermine its chances for surviving.

I don't measure my life with money. How can I? Lack of money is one hell of a reason to commit suicide. If ever I earn one million dollars, I would make sure my daughter would study with the best teachers in the world, no matter how far away they might be. Only then would I pay back the debts I have accumulated through publishing.

On Publishing

My experience has been too negative for me to continue pretending that everything is cheerful in the world of publishing. Not that I was ever cheerful or optimistic about my profession; I never was, and I can be quite an optimistic person in private. If I am bitter and always complaining about my work, it is perhaps because from the start I was pushed into a situation that I did not want to be in. (No, this is not cynicism: in a recent book on the history of Canadian publishing, its author does not even mention a press that has been around for over twenty-five years and has more than 300 titles in its catalogue: Guernica Editions.)

I had chosen to be a filmmaker, but financial constraints led me to switch to publishing instead. If I speak of economy, it is because I believe that Andy Warhol and François Truffaut were both right in stressing the fact that art is bound by the question of money. Vanity, egoism, egotism are short-lived pleasures that leave an open wound in your heart, as well as your bank account.

There is no money to be made by selling books as an independent publisher. Seventy percent of our sales go into the very well-organized distribution and bookstore industries. Even when we sell 1000 copies of *The Voices We Carry* edited by Mary Jo Bona, or 750 copies of Viscusi's *Astoria,* I am not able to pay back the production costs of the books. In the case of Viscusi's book, which brought in $11,250, 70% of this amount (that is $7,875) went to distributors and booksellers. That left Guernica with an income of $3,375. Viscusi's book cost me about $10,000 to produce, which means that I found myself $6,625 in the red, even though I sold out of this book. This is the reality of the industry.

Publishing books is more a cultural duty than a money venture. It is the game of rich communities. Guernica is not about publishing books. There are too many presses out there which do just that. Guernica does not publish books; it discovers authors and promotes these published authors. Guernica is in many ways a movement.

I published my first book in 1973 because no one else would publish it. A first book with its faults and immaturity. Its defects could easily have been corrected with the guidance of a sensitive editor. So I started to look for a publisher interested in me. When, in 1975, I did manage to find a good editor, the publishing house went under. And since 1975 I have seen a number of presses fold. Small publishing houses fold when they only publish books, and not authors. Large presses use books like tissue paper.

I have come to understand that as a writer, if I want to publish, and if I want to publish with a press that will survive, I have to work with a press that promises me longevity, a press that represents a literary movement, a cultural happening. When I finally do find such a press, I decide to work with that press for as long as possible.

As soon as my French publisher was sold to a large multinational, all that movement died. When that publisher became a publisher of books and no longer a literary movement, my desire to publish with that press (and in that language: it was a French-language press) came to an end. I was not the only writer to feel this way; there were many of us.

It is natural that we expect the editor to surround us with other writers who share a common experience. We write in a similar way; we express similar concepts and project a shared world vision. We read one another and quote one another's texts, review one another's books. It is this that pushes us to incredible heights of literary joy.

On the English-language front, this sort of complicity did not exist in the 1970s, nor did it really exist in the 1990s. This is why I was "forced" to create Guernica, which has become a haven for writers who feel and share a common vision. There is, therefore, no need for another press that offers the same sort of services. If there is, then I might as well put an end to Guernica. I am doing this work because there is a need for it in our intellectual community. As soon as that need vanishes, so does the job. I am telling you that the need is still there, however, and to meddle with this need is to bring to an end what is still very unstable, even after twenty-five years of existence. Publishing presses come of age after fifty years of existence.

Two things are certain: being a publisher or editor are tasks I will stop caring for if another press repeats what we are already doing, or if our intellectuals rush off elsewhere to get their books published. Why re-invent the wheel?

Integrity is what brings respect to the intellectuals of a community. How do we expect to be respected if we do not respect ourselves? And we don't respect ourselves, or if we do, we only do so superficially.

For me this job is neither a source of egotistic pleasure, nor a source of financial gain. It is a tough twenty-four hour job that never enables me to seduce anyone, nor get seduced. I depend on other intellectuals for their input and fidelity. I have lost three wives since 1978, the year I founded Guernica. I have lost and keep losing friends and a lot of precious money every day of the year. These twenty-five years have darkened any light that I might have noticed out there in the distance. I really believe that, contrary to appearances, our feel for a community might be coming to an end. And we are to blame.

To be a publisher is an occupation which is defined by world standards. UNESCO and the world community dictate these standards, and to pretend otherwise is foolish and vain. If we are publishers, then we are expected to abide by these world standard rules. I am tempted to elaborate on foolishness and vanity, but I won't. This would necessitate hours of blabbing which I no longer care for.

Copyright infringement is one important aspect of these rules, and there has been copyright infringement against publishers lately. Often vanity is what places many published writers in the delicate situation of copyright infringement. But then again, even when copyright has been infringed upon, who has the money to take the culprit to court? Copyright issues prove to me that there are no equal standards for artists. Some have more rights than others.

If publishers wanted to, they could sue a number of writers for breaking their contracts. I don't mean to point fingers. I am simply trying to open our eyes to what is happening on a professional level to our infrastructure and how our vanity is in fact starting to gnaw away at any possible growth in a serious superstructure.

Copyright is a legal matter, and a very serious matter which should concern us all. If we do not concern ourselves with copyright matters, then we can't expect other communities to respect our community. As a publisher, this puts me in a very delicate situation. I am not sure what to do. To make sure that copyright material is protected requires money, not egoism. There are many examples.

A portion of a book is reprinted by another press. Who has the financial means to take this second publisher to court? Large segments of books are being photocopied and there is no way to track down (a) these copyright infringements, (b) monies that rightfully belong to the authors and publisher.

Authors are publishing elsewhere when they themselves have signed contracts that advised them not to. Many will start defending themselves by giving a number of valid reasons. What will happen when we all start acting that way – as some often do in the "interest" of their work?

Should publishers start taking their authors to court?

What will happen when other publishers willingly take advantage of us all without even telling us that they are using our works? Recently I found out that a press had stolen sections from one of Guernica's books without even mentioning its source. The issues do not affect me on a personal level; they affect all authors.

Rule number one: know your rights. Whenever another publisher asks you to participate in a book, make sure that there is no copyright infringement. When I say publisher, I mean book publisher, or any project that entails the publication of a book outside of your publisher or whichever company you have signed with.

To publish in a magazine does not entail the same procedures. If another book publisher asks you to publish, you have to ask your original publisher to "free" you. Not doing so might mean that you are breaking your contract.

In turn, you can sue the second publisher for leading you into breaking your contract. If you sign two contracts, then you will find yourself in the worst of possible situations. Without copyright enforcement, there is no cultural community.

Unfortunately, until we see the end of regionalism we will witness more destruction and pain. It is regional chauvinism that prevents ethnic communities of the world from connecting with one another.

We have to think of ourselves as borderless people, and I don't believe we are able to do so under the present circumstances that we have created for ourselves. Every day we fall into quagmires set before us by opportunists. It is only by acting intelligently and diligently that we will survive as an intellectual community. Of course, the prerequisite to this is a desire among the members of this community to see its intellectuals survive.

Newspapers and magazines have a major role in the survival of a cultural group. A publisher depends on them for its well-being. I am not a magazine publisher. Magazine and newspaper publishers are a very lively bunch of men and women, and I envy them. But I do not have that sense of adventure. So I will never be a magazine publisher, even though I am one of the founders of a magazine called *Vice Versa*. I can only point to the important role that magazines should play in our global community, a role that is only shyly embraced at the present moment.

In my opinion, there are two types of magazines: one that situates itself *before* book publishing, and the other that comes *after*. One that announces a new author; the second that promotes this author's published book. In between is the publisher.

Though these types of magazines may appear to differ in the thematic services they render, they both promise in essence one basic benefit: the promotion of men and women from within a specific community.

On rare occasions a magazine attains such a level of success that it is able to embrace a number of communities; usually, a magazine can only concentrate on one community at a time.

When I look at the Italic communities in North America, I am a little surprised to see the waste of energy. This is why I have decided to become firmly outspoken against our community's magazines. Petty regionalisms, naive prejudices, and peacock foolishness are preventing our magazines from doing their job.

Not *Vice Versa*, not *Via,* not *Italian Americana*, not *Italian Canadiana*, not *Differentia*, not *Eyetalian* – none of these are (were) doing what must (had to) be done. They are all stepping on one another's shoes. There is confusion of purposes, as I see it, and it is this confusion that upsets the normal flow of events. It is about time they get together and start building up a transnational team of expert editors. No hockey team, no soccer team can ever expect to win a game if all its members are goalies or defense persons. Every team needs certain specialists, and it is the organization of these specialists that will bring a team to victory.

Instead of magazine editors sitting down together and planning out a cultural strategy, they have fallen into the political agenda of nationalism – which is to purposefully keep communities divided by any means possible. Divided, we have no strength left to analyze the reality outside the fifteen-minute glory that a cute article kindles for us.

Neither before- nor after-book publication services are truly offered. There is ambiguity of purpose and this is why we are unable to step out of the pit we are trapped in. As a publisher of authors this is a concern for me. Our authors are not spoken about, or when they are spoken about, the words (of praise or criticism) are so scarce that nothing culturally powerful will ever come from them. In fact, the situation is so bad that we can't even agree to compliment a fine writer. No wonder we need outside approbation to congratulate an author.

There are so few books being produced that it should be quite easy to coach a great campaign of positive and concerted reviews and promotional tours. Where are the press agents and lawyers who are fundamental to the smooth flow of information? Right now we are spending thousands of dollars which generate nothing but silence. And overexposure of single authors is another, more subtle form of silence.

Instead of being centrifugal, most of our magazines are centripetal; they are constantly moving inwards, instead of pushing outwards. Hence, the silence of our works; hence, the silence of our presence. And if the silence ever gets broken, it is because someone *outside* the community chooses to make good use of our products for his or her own purposes. And when this occurs, we suddenly all find something to scream about. Be it good or bad, at that point, it really does not matter anymore. It all amounts to the same ugly emotion – envy – for discovery did not spring from within, but from without.

Every time this happens we are tossed back to square one: regionalism is killing our intellectual community. Many start the race, but few ever make it to the finish line. And the few who do make it, don't have much energy left for those left behind. I am interested, not in the race, but in making sure that we have the training to swim to and fro in the river of literature.

You should read the sort of query letters I get from Italian writers. All of them say one thing: "Eh, you, ignorant fool, when are you going to publish me?" My archives, which amount to over one hundred boxes of titillating documents, are rotting away in my warehouses; they will attest to what I say. It is unbelievable that people can actually think they can get away with discourtesy.

This sort of unacceptable attitude is possible only because we do not take ourselves seriously. We don't understand how many years of cultural suffering it has taken for our community to arrive at this point in our existence. We have newspapers, magazines, and publishing houses. It is arrogance on our part to think that these can come about again, were they to disappear. They won't. The inventiveness that created them will never again be. If Guernica dies, there will never be another Guernica, another home for the authors of our community. Our works will be scattered and slowly vanish into nothingness. I cannot repeat it often enough: there are more important issues than the vain desire of re-inventing what is already there. What we must worry about is how we use what is here to the best of our capacities for the betterment and survival of our cultural communities.

The Future of Italic Culture

People often ask me what role Italian culture plays in America, and each time I am inclined to respond by saying, "None." That would be a bad joke, with a grain of truth in it. Before giving a serious answer, we would have to define what Italian culture is. Can we appropriately define Italian culture? We describe it, but we can't define it.

First things first. We have to detach *culture* from *country*. I prefer to speak of the Italic culture, instead of the culture one encounters in Italy. The Italic culture is the highest level of culture for things Italian. Italic culture is to Italy what *francophonie* is to France: something that lies both within and outside its borders. If Italic culture does in fact exist in North, Central, and South America, it surely does not have the role that an "official" culture has. To play it safe, I could say that the Italian culture one finds on the American continents is the lifestyle the emigrant carried from Italy in his suitcase and memory. What happens when whatever it was that he carried from abroad starts going adrift is that it gets replaced by nostalgia.

Nostalgia – a sentiment of wanting what has been lost forever – is not the same thing as memory, nor does it resemble what the emigrant carried in his suitcase. A culture of nostalgia is alive and well in America, strangely enough, more in Canada than in the U.S.A., where a huge gap opened between first-generation emigrants and the subsequent generations of men and women born on American soil.

In Canada that hole is not present. Italians in Canada luckily find themselves only a few degrees separated from Italy. There were no overt laws, like in other countries, that forbade the massive influx of new immigrants who kept the flame of culture burning. This is why I stubbornly refuse to say that a culture of nostalgia has replaced a living culture. I am critical of proponents of nostalgia because they make an argument for something that does not truly exist in general. Nostalgia in this country is fiction, stuff for operettas. How are we to experience nostalgia if we have lost nothing?

The Italic culture is about to be recognized worldwide. It all depends on Italians around the world. Despite the diminishing numbers of immigrants arriving from Italy – which I hope is due to a drop in emigration from Italy and not a tactic of Canadian anti-Italian immigration policy – Italians who establish themselves in this country straighten up what needs to be tidied up in the communities. They untangle the webs that have darkened memory in the minds of those who have been living here for decades or for a century, some of whom were treated as *enemy aliens* during World War II. (To learn about the experience of imprisonment in an internment camp in Petawawa, Ontario, I recommend *Ville sans femmes* by Mario Duliani – the book has been translated into English by Antonino Mazza.)

The Italian culture in America (as experienced by

immigrants and their off-spring born on American soil) is about Italians attempting, by all means necessary, to live their lifestyle fully, without nostalgia. Sporadically, fear prevents some from doing so. For many, keeping their culture alive is a continuous battle against demoralization and subtle manifestations of bullying. There is not a single day when an Italian is not asked, in one form or another, "When are you going to become American? Soon I hope. If not, beware."

I use the term *American* in its widest sense: people from North, Central, and South America. When we are dealing with American pluricultural realities, there is no special way of differentiating the countries in this part of the world, regardless of their distinct histories. Each one treats its minorities, more or less, in a similar manner.

In Canada, the British, French, and First Nations are protected by federal laws. In reality, though, there are basically two official Canadian peoples: the British and the French. All the others are merged into what is commonly known as multicultural communities; Natives have been granted inches of privilege. Quickly the immigrant who sets foot on Canadian soil must choose which side he wants to live on: the British or the French? The real decision is whether to choose Canadian monarchy or an independent Quebec.

This policy of limited options produces its share of contradictions. One cannot choose both sides. I tried. It's an impossibility in political terms. (Though one could very well be for an independent Canadian Pluricultural Republic.) The fact of the matter is that Canada is heading towards an unavoidable political crisis. For the first time in its history, the majority of the Canadian population is neither British nor French.

This demographic disequilibrium, the redistribution of power among the minority communities, will irremediably provoke a major political tremor within the next generation or so. If Quebec were to successfully separate, the departure of the majority of francophones would transform the British and its powers into a minority group in a land where the populace would be holding onto rights not legally ratified. Dare we say this: Canada could become an apartheid-like society?

In the U.S.A., where no such dominating cultural group is possible, this demographic challenge presents itself differently. Multiculturalism, in the U.S.A., excludes most people without "color." Yet this is where their Trojan horse awaits. There, the future question will be: "Who has what rights?" and "Which group has more rights than the others?"

If only those groups said to belong to multicultural communities are protected by civil rights, what rights can those other cultural groups who do not fit under the multicultural umbrella claim? Are they all, as is currently suggested, "whites?" And that question will entail other troubling questions: "What is this thing called the white race? What does it stand for?"

We know through experience that time changes the meaning of words, that he who was once a black person will be classified as white. As is the case of Italians, who were for many years considered by the press as "black" folk. Where will such "declassified" persons fit in the grand cultural mosaic?

Italians have been pushed up the social ladder, that is true; they have been, so to speak, liberated, cleared of the pejorative connotations attached to ethnicity. Still, one little detail does carry over from their "black" history: they never were granted, in exchange for this freedom, any concrete power or honor normally associated with dominant classes. Italians might own houses and expensive sport cars, but they do not have their own schools. Are we to conclude then that Italians bartered their black status for the right to become British?

Like cultures on other continents, American culture is an instrument very few can fiddle around with. Culture belongs to national establishments. The bilingual and bicultural Canada teachers taught me about at school does not exist. Not only is there no such thing as a cultural transference from one cultural and linguistic group to another, neither is it true that Canada is bilingual and bicultural. For many years, the fact that, as an editor, I published books in both official languages was perceived as heresy. Being a trilingual and tricultural person, I decided one day to transplant my tricultural baggage to a new cultural center, away from Montreal, which had been my cultural center for over forty years.

Moving to Toronto, I told myself, would bring me closer to an Italian center. That was not the case. Toronto is one of the largest Italian cities in the world. Yet we never hear of the achievements of Italians on the news (except, of course, when these have to do with organized crime) or in any other official cultural institution. Like I said, Canada has its contradictions. Injustice is everywhere the same. No nation expects to see its culture blossom outside of its borders. That would mean the demise of the nation. This is the last thing on a nation's wish list. Ethnics are given little choice: they have to work in English. Why English? (The Plains of Abraham?) Your guess is as good as mine, but I imagine that it has something to do with the English language being, sadly enough, the largest linguistic prison in which groups like Italians can breathe in.

It is a mistake to place language on the same plane as culture. Culture spans way beyond the fields of language. Any culture aspiring to survive in this era will have to open its borders and visit the new horizons appearing in the distance. Culture must be centrifugal. The Italic is, fortunately, a culture beyond a country.

Statistics claim that there are over sixty million people in the world who speak Italian. We also know that these numbers are insufficient to keep any language alive. According to certain anthropologists, no language will survive if it is not spoken, on a daily basis, by at least 150 million people. If these figures prove to be correct, then we can mournfully deduce that the Italian language is doomed.

Italy cannot, alone, as the kernel of the Italian language, carry the burden of survival. No country with such a small population can. This is why Italy must encourage Italians living abroad to learn to speak Italian.

The main obstacle to this reform, if we can call it that, is that the Italian language might be unsuitable for

ANTONIO D'ALFONSO

expressing the complexities of the lifestyles foaming in Italic culture. For millions of Italics, the Italian language simply does not correspond to anything concrete in their everyday life. This is a major stumbling block. Italy has, until now, been reticent about recognizing the existence of Italics abroad, whether for politic reasons or for fear of meddling in another country's affairs. Does that mean that Italy considers these people unimportant to the cause?

Italy should study what its neighbors have accomplished with respect to cultural matters: France, Germany, England, Portugal, Spain have all had to accept cultural decentralization in order to survive. In the short term, Italy must be ready to accept Italics abroad, regardless of the language they speak or the country they live in. There is no other antidote to the blight. The Italian language will have to become secondary for the time being, just as it was at the time of the unification of Italy. We have to thank television if Italians started to make Italian their mother/father tongue. By embracing the Italic paradigm, language will surely be promoted to a priority. But first Italics around the world must unite on the cultural front, and make the Italic culture their main cause, not Italy, nor its language.

We constantly return to square one: the *brouhaha* over what Italic culture is. What mental image could possibly bring together people who share a common heritage yet live in different parts of the world? What could this common denominator be? Language? Certainly not. Nationalism? Certainly not.

There are more Italians living abroad than there are

Italians in Italy; more Italians born outside of Italy than Italians in Italy. Religion? Italians are Christian, Jewish, Muslim, Buddhist, atheist. Cuisine? Italians can be vegetarian or meat-eaters. So what is it that constitutes this Italic culture that fascinates so many? Piero Bassetti, in a 2002 interview with Sergio Roic, suggests lifestyle.

That might be one answer, though I am not certain many Italics would want to live the life I live. There is no answer, and there might never be an answer. Perhaps the lack of reason for wanting to unite at all makes Italics who they are. Who can tell?

Acceptance of ignorance has never prevented Italics from being proud of their culture throughout the centuries. Their culture is a dream that never comes true.

Artists and musicians have tried to foster some intelligent explanation; so have writers. We are now waiting for what linguists, sociologists, and anthropologists have to show us. This inter-disciplinary meeting of the minds may help us unearth the minerals on which will be founded this federation of Italic peoples. Cesare Pavese wrote: "It is not Italy I love, but the Italian people." That should serve as the motto for all Italics. The foundation of their culture is immaterial, for it is countryless.

Too often Italy regards the foreign part of the Italic culture as being primarily nostalgic in character. This attitude shows deliberate signs of paternalism and carelessness. There is a world that divides nostalgia and active memory. Many people abroad persist in considering themselves Italians. Let's call them all Italics.

We should also immediately redefine Italic literature. There are two main branches: 1. the literature written in standard Italian; 2. the literature written in other languages (English, French, German, Portuguese, Spanish, and Italic dialects). If we are unable to accept such a view of Italic literature, then it is useless to proceed with this talk about a unifying culture. This reclassification of creative works is mandatory. Is all literature written in Italian, for instance, substantially Italic? Aren't translations just bridges to the understanding of other cultures? Likewise, do the works produced by Italic writers living outside Italy, written in many languages, necessarily embody the cultures to which these languages belong?

Many works might very well fit into the Italic culture, even though they have been written in a foreign language. There are two thematic offshoots at the present moment: 1. works that propose the death of Italic culture (those that trade in the Italic culture for another); 2. works that painfully tear themselves away from the body of the culture that gave them birth (Italian, English, French, German, Spanish, Portuguese, Italic dialects) in order to integrate into another culture, a redefining culture, one more cosmopolitan and universal.

Much of the interest for things Italic is passing, superficial. There will be a day when the leaning tower of Pisa and pasta will become outdated, of no particular interest. This is true for Italics as well as for their neighbors. Participation in cultural manifestations should not only be a question of fashion. Young men and women frequently demonstrate their pride of being Italian, unaware of the social responsibilities these

group statements suppose. One shouldn't express affir-
mations of a cultural nature without thinking. They
might backfire and bother the neighbors or confuse the
politicians. Behind all this display of fervor cringes an
Italic culture which is in crisis everywhere.

Remedies that will heal the stress of an impaired
identity are not easy to come by. Italy has done little to
offer help. Italians in Italy are too grounded in their earth
to care about what tales are unfolding abroad. Italic culture needs to adopt a new spirit, free of the refurbished
nationalist habits of Italy. Only an Italic commonwealth
can pull its culture out of disintegration.

Alter rem, alter valorem

One the thing, the other the value of the thing.
Christopher Marlowe

Modern-day nationalists are interested only in the destructive forces that ethnic difference can unleash. When they talk about the right to self-determination, they mean their right to determine who will be allowed to survive on their territory, and who will not.

Hans Magnus Enzensberger,
Civil War

A national culture is highly political. A nation's network of mass media has a precise agenda to follow: to keep alive or protect its culture; to destroy anything that will belittle, impoverish, disintegrate, or kill that culture either from the inside or out.

It would be naive to believe that culture is philanthropically open to difference. National cultures will accept only what they can assimilate within their boundaries and immediately reject the rest.

In Europe, nations are presently seeking to close their borders in order to make an old dream come true; that is, to unify regional differences and to create a new supranational culture. They attract whatever acceptable elements of neighboring cultures from within and outside their geographical territory and, of course, make sure to expel all undesirable elements of foreign culture.

So as to achieve this harmonious marriage of the known and the unknown, Europe must first transform its nations into countries, which is no easy task. Though capital may easily function beyond borders, national cultures can't. This denationalization of Europe is responsible for incredible political turbulence, as we have seen, since this sort of political activity, suitable for finance, goes against the very grain of European history when it comes to issues of culture and politics.

The metamorphosis is far from being simple and straightforward. The absence of homogeneity in the regional makeup of any one country makes this shifting of identity problematic and often dangerous. The events that tore Yugoslavia apart are harsh reminders of the difficulties involved in trying to define who is what and where. The creation of supranational myths continues to push countries into the well of nightmares.

Because no country in the Americas is a nation in the true sense of the word, the struggle for cultural preeminence has been exceedingly violent and has been executed with extreme shrewdness.

Nevertheless, cultural preponderance was never and is not a divine right. North, South, and Central America are composed of pluriethnic and pluricultural societies that no melting pot philosophy of *tabula rasa* will satisfy. Whether one likes it or not, pluriculturalism demands the serious attention of serious minds.

The U.S.A. is no exception. Perhaps, had the Confederates won the Civil War, things would have turned out differently for pro-nationalists. We will never know. One thing is sure: the hatred and xenophobic movements, as they exist in the North America, are devoid of nationalist beliefs. Their actions arise more from a well-orchestrated, gang-spirited racial and religious intolerance than a philosophy based on nationhood as we find in Europe. Bigots are as much an obstacle to democracy as are nationalists.

Ethnicity in the Americas challenges cultural dynasties. More than an intellectual defiance, ethnicity is above all an economic and political threat, for it menaces the distribution of power and capital from within. Capital need not be centralized as it used to be in the past; it can accommodate parallel networks. The centralization of culture is being taken to task by minority groups everywhere.

A nation's art market is closely tied to national culture. This entails an overt agenda which seldom plays in the favor of minority artworks. No wonder then that national markets are targeted by ethnicity. The breakdown of nationalism spares no level of society: capital, law, education, religion, and culture are affected by the fall of walls.

More than from outside enemy forces, the nation-state is being threatened and attacked from within. Because nations have become so busy protecting their own interior cultural "black holes," they have been quite ineffectual when it comes to offering assistance to endangered neighboring nations.

Every state is so busy patching up its collapsing citadels that its citizens are pretty much left on their own. How do we make sure that this interior political turmoil does not dissolve into chaos? The immediate response is the creation of a police force so potent that the state turns into a police military state. Are Western nation-states free of such an outcome?

We must be able to accept compromise without giving in to intellectual blackmail. Every intellectual, whether he or she is aware of it or not, plays a role in the cultural scheme of things. The rules of classification are dictated from the power elites and not one person is exempted from the games of national traditions. Awakening to the machinations of power can be disastrous for many. This is of urgent concern for every intellectual on all sides of the political spectrum and of every affiliation.

How to avoid the real demise of peace and outbreak of civil unrest? In order to assure citizens everywhere peace and well-being, it has become essential for states to maintain equal opportunity for their citizens. But, as we are learning from the U.S.A., there are always forces that undermine the need for equal opportunity.

Equal opportunity in the world of art, though it is accompanied by financial balms, does not necessarily guarantee social acceptance. Books by minority groups, for instance, may get published thanks to grants and private sponsors, but they rarely receive proper coverage by the media or, if they are spoken about, are categorized, often lambasted, and reduced to their smallest denominator, to the degree that they become devoid of any cultural value.

What we are left with is nothing more than generalizations and insignificant babbling, and one wonders if silence and indifference would not have been better responses from critics.

Even when a reviewer writes trivialities such as, "It is the work of an Native American, an Italian German, an Arab Frenchman, therefore not universal," they manage to denaturalize the work of its context. The thing is allowed to exist, but it has been emptied of its value. One is right in asking, "Where has the value of the thing vanished to?"

The cultures of the Americas have never been national in the way that European cultures have been national. When American regional cultures lower themselves by imitating and acting under the influence of European nationalisms, America loses something of its essence.

Not that European cultures should not be emulated, perhaps they should, but the trouble is that each time America impersonates European culture, it ends up looking like a caricature of the real thing.

To avoid being cast as total imbeciles we should foster our unique brand of cultural products, products that are free of nationalism in all its disguises and that will promote peace and understanding among minorities, first in America and then in Europe.

Though North America is not unique in the world

in possessing pluricultural realities, what we do have that many other continents with pluriethnic communities do not is a capitalist and imperialist "democracy."

Evidently, to counteract the paralysis in which many European countries find themselves, they are now trying to stretch beyond their boundaries in order to bridge themselves with neighboring cultures and find common denominators among distinct societies. They seem to want to become more American in this way; that is, less national and more pluricultural. But there is a lot of work still to be done.

The problem right now in Europe is that politicians are quickly discovering that the nations they thought were coherent and strong are starting to show their true face in public: Italy, Germany, France, England, Spain, Greece are more fragile than expected. The national glue is letting go. What many believed was one thing is showing itself to be another thing all together.

It became obvious in the 1990s that forming a supranational Europe risked creating havoc by splitting individual countries asunder. Separatist movements are suddenly becoming stronger all over Europe. This unexpected outcome might well entail even stranger side-effects in the future.

Separatist movements, if successful in their demands for self-determination, will need to work much harder to maintain a level of economic and cultural standing that will make them acceptable to a united Europe. Separation that might be profitable in the short term may become a serious handicap in the long run. Will small nations, with their ethnic black holes, be able to afford the cost of keeping their position in a united federation? This is the gamble that separatist groups must take.

It is against this backdrop of deteriorating borders and identity that are wakened the specter of mass markets and the industry of aggressive promotion of national art.

Does the world need to be reminded of the true nature of art, whereby only "high art" is valuable and the rest of the production discouraged from leaving the ghettos of select groups?

In reality what occurs whenever a state's media industry grins is that we notice the incredible amount of struggle involved in order to maintain a national cultural tradition alive and well.

Why should there be this urgent need to reassure a population of the value of its national traditions?

In matters of culture, if one needs to be reassured that things are all right, more often than not this means that serious irreparable damage to national culture has already been done.

At the same time as a state's press is telling its population "Hey, we've got great writers," journalists all over are writing articles denouncing the presence of too many books on the market. They warn people that too many books on the market reduce both the quality and the appreciation of the works produced. Danger signals are popping up everywhere to announce the end of an era. What is in fact this doom that is being foretold? Is something really dying, or is this simply adaptation to a new world order that is evolving? There are two reasons for this prediction of doom:

1. The power elites are feeling threatened: no national power elite wishes to forego its control on culture.

2. The death of the mass market: monolithic mainstream culture is being divided by the gradual emergence of parallel markets, a network of small commercial centers not affiliated to large financial conglomerates.

The call for control of publications is but one way of ridding the state of undesirables. Other ways are:

1. Reviving past glories so that money can return to the pockets of elites that often own the rights of major works in their tradition.

2. Commissioning new works that fulfill the needs of new and burgeoning ethnic markets.

3. In the meantime, cultural power elites must keep the mirage of a unified nation alive. They must continue offering its newly arrived citizens the hope of a better future, and that future will become better on the sole condition that they work *within* the nation-state and not *outside* it.

Unfortunately, the philanthropy of benefactors of the arts is often limited: Only a handful of writers out of the entire lot of writers rising from ethnic ghettos will be chosen. There is only so much change a nation can assimilate in a short period of time.

There is no better manner to vent one's hatred on an immediate enemy than by luring one of the enemy to the other side.

This encouragement for a better world will turn into competition for ethnic writers. Ferociously, almost overnight, they will turn against one another.

It would be idealistic to believe that a national culture would recognize and reward a member of its enemy clan. The enemy will always be the enemy. No two ways about this. The quickest method of ridding oneself of the enemy is by instigating infighting.

If it is violence that the state is after, no need for it to indulge in fighting itself; all that is needed is to incite hatred among minorities and encourage hatred and anger to be channeled against minorities instead of the state, the true enemy.

The most insidious way to demolish a group of ethnic writers is to recognize the talent of one to the detriment of all the others.

The jealousy and envy among the spurned writers will suffice to kindle a major clan war.

The power elite of the nation might be aware of a possible dwindling of its market. Not that the original members of the clan are not reproducing as quickly as desired, but that the market seems unable to integrate new citizens fast enough, nor do these new citizens show any willingness to integrate into mainstream national culture.

Yet the nation-state finds itself forced to attract new

membership from groups of people that either do not wish to join, or from groups it has till now found undesirable.

But membership in national culture is never altruistic. New membership is summoned by invitation only: either from a minority inside its borders or from a neighboring nation-state.

What we have at work is a continuous tug of war, a pushing away and pulling in of men and women. Who decides who enters? Who is pushed away? Who is pulled inside?

One is either being pulled to the center of the nation-state or one is being pushed away from it. No one can be in both places at once. One cannot be the other.

This manipulation of allegiances has affected our ways of defining the status of the writer. The paradox is that the last thing any writer wishes is to be classified and boxed in a category. Nevertheless, this is exactly what is being done.

What we see today, with rare exceptions, are persons who pretend to be one thing and are in reality something else. Analyze most of the works that are being given recognition and you will soon notice that many of these products advance, in their own particular way, the cause of the nation-state.

Culture must be at once conscious and unconscious; it must be desired but not controlled, we must want it to be thriving but not artificially alive with gadgets. Culture is a living organism that is capable of giving and receiving from the inside as well as from the outside.

If a culture is no longer cherished, it is futile to continue discussing ways of getting it to survive. If all intellectuals do is foolishly brandish their clan's badge and flag in the face of people who couldn't care less who they are, then they should not be surprised to see their culture vanish totally from the face of the world.

During this past decade there has been much talk in certain circles of ethnic writing and minority perspectives. Yet there seems to be no consensus of what it means exactly to be an ethnic. In America, I mean all of the Americas – North, Central, and South America – individual identity is usually synonymous with anti-nationalism. (Somehow anti-nationalistic sentiments get perverted by strange forms of patriotism.) So why is there this sudden awakening of ethnicities as well as a deep resentment to the very idea of ethnicity? It must be that instinctively people are aware that love of one's culture does not consequently imply the love of nation.

We assume therefore that there is a real need to discuss, for example, Italian culture, and that this need is both desired and heartfelt by many people across the world, outside of Italy.

Unhappily, most of what is considered Italian is usually considered an offshoot of something else, often of a major national culture. This is a mistake.

When we label products as being Italian, are we referring to European culture or American culture? If we reply both, we are deluding ourselves since European culture has demonstrated no sign of including

Italian works abroad in their national canons. And if we reply American, what proof do we have that these works have been accepted by North American standards?

The real question to ask is: "Do we really wish to reduce the pluricultural realities of America to European nationalist loyalties and vice versa, European realities to invented American national culture?" When we speak of hybrid cultures this is what is implied.

Some will nevertheless question us: "Shouldn't Italian culture be considered primarily an offshoot of European culture, since Italy belongs to the European tradition?"

If this is the case then, when we say that Italian culture is part of the European supraculture, can we expect it to be open enough to accept the Italic experience outside of Italy?

So far Europe has not shown any willingness to integrate the works of European writers living abroad. It will accept writers who left only if they were recognized before their departure. Migration too is codified: one cannot leave without first receiving a stamp from the national customs officers. A person can criticize a culture, but never another nation. This requisite removes the resoluteness of modern emigration, leading us to imagine emigration as a dated phenomenon, something with a beginning and an end. Sociologists have repeated the truism: poverty is never a good enough reason to emigrate.

The truth of the matter is that emigration is an intrinsically human characteristic: nomads existed from the beginning, from the rise of the *homo sapiens*. So why this sudden sense of punishment from the mother nation-state?

Is this idea of emigration and motherland the path to follow in order to understand what one is saying when one speaks of writing with Italian references or claims a right to be Italian?

Maybe we are neither interested in European culture nor Italic culture at all, and only care for our own individual territorial exceptions, whereby Italian Americans, for example, are just British writers with Italian names and stories. Are these distinctions perfectly useless? Some intellectuals repeat *yes*, since what counts for them in the end is the stamp of approval that the host places on our work.

Others will disagree saying that questions of emigration, ethnicity, and nationhood are fundamental, since without the answers to these questions we will precipitate into oblivion the successes that have been achieved till now.

There are various branches of the Italic experience in the world which can be detailed as follows.

Category 1: The Europeans

1. The writer living in Italy who writes in Italian.
2. The writer living in Italy who writes in a dialect.
3. The writer living in Italy who writes in a language that is neither Italian nor a dialect of Italy.

The Europeans

No one would argue with us for an instant if we stated that Pier Paolo Pasolini and Eduardo De Filippo are Italian, but what happens in the case of Ezra Pound? Why isn't Pound considered an Italian writer? He lived in Italy for decades. Obviously territorial rights were not enough in Pound's case to grant him the status of being an Italian writer. Language plays a major role in the national culture of Italy. Some national cultures are indeed stubborn.

Category 2: The Italics

1. The writer living outside of Italy who writers in Italian (Giose Rimanelli, Filippo Salvatore).

2. The writer living outside of Italy who writers in a dialect (Corrado Mastropasqua).

3. The writer living outside of Italy who writes in a foreign language (Len Gasparini in Canada, Eugene Mirabelli in the U.S.A., Gino Chiellino in Germany).

The Italics

In which tradition do Rimanelli, Salvatore, and Mastro-pasqua fit? In the Italian, the American, the Canadian or the Quebecois tradition?

These three writers were published in Italy yet none figures in Italian national anthologies. They are published in English- and French-language anthologies, despite the fact that they write in Italian.

Contrary to the Europeans, for the Italics, territorial identification takes precedence over the use of language.

The same applies to Gasparini, Mirabelli, and Chiellino. Pluriethnic cultures prove to be more open, since language is not a valid motive for excluding people.

It would be, however, a fatal mistake to deduct from the faded stamp of approval that total membership of writers into the tradition is granted by any one nation.

Acceptance cannot be measured by the degree of fame or recognition initially received by any one writer or group of writers. Success is the issue here, and true success for the ethnic writer is survival of the writer's works beyond the writer's lifetime. What guarantee do we have that the works of these writers will survive even a decade?

There is so much disagreement between those writers entrenched in the belief that language defines culture and those others who, though they might have a culture, possess no language they can call their own.

One of my hypotheses is that the Italic culture, if reduced to individual compartments (countries), stands a good chance of disappearing sooner than imagined. If taken globally, the Italic culture has the necessary tools to produce a tradition of its own.

Whether this literary production will stand on its own, whether it will be forced into a larger world tradition, or whether it will be downsized to a minor movement in a larger tradition is still to be seen.

Productions themselves are not sufficient to withstand the indifference of time. A concerted effort from everyone across the world will be required for the products to find a permanent home.

There is one major problem: writers without a

language. Languageless writers are plagued. Writers who write in one language with the hope of being accepted by the tradition of another culture are the individuals who require the most support.

If we are to accept T.S. Eliot's definition of a great poet – "The truly great poet makes his language a great language" – then ethnic writers might never make it beyond the time-span of a single decade. This is a pity since these writers are the ones who carry the culture on their shoulders for the rest of the population.

Ethnicity is more a question of structure than content – once imitation of stories is made possible, there is no more need for the real thing. Only the value of the thing counts, and that value is what capital is most interested in.

How can one emulate a writer who has no language? Yet it is the writer without a language, who permits art to cross over to life and makes it impossible for art-works to be appropriated and recuperated. It is the writer without a language who serves as a beacon for future generations of writers. But this is the exception, not the rule.

We have chosen the following six types of writers to help define, in one way or another, what it means or what it doesn't mean to be a writer today.

There are two main categories: the *National Writer* and the *Ethnic Writer.*

The National Writer

1. The national writer who uses positive elements of an ethnic culture in his or her work.

2. The national writer who uses negative elements of an ethnic culture in his or her work.

3. The national writer who does not use elements of an ethnic culture.

The National Writer 3

Let us start by discarding number three of this category since a writer who does not use the activities from other groups does not concern us at the present moment.

The National Writer 2

The national writer who uses ethnic images is of particular interest to us for two reasons: people applaud the writer who boasts things ethnic, and condemn the writer who ridicules things ethnic.

More often than not it is the writer who speaks negatively about things ethnic who grabs our attention most powerfully.

Why does a writer use a certain type of character and what role does this ethnic character play in the development of the plot?

Many ethnic communities will not stand for this badmouthing of their heritage by other ethnic groups. They are fast to point their judging index fingers at writers who smear in public the reputation of their collectivity.

But should we be surprised by the negativity of some national writers towards a particular ethnic culture? Not really, it's part of being human. No one is expected to be all loving in this world of ours. Many writers mirror the emotions of how a large portion of the national population feels about certain aspects of their society.

The National Writer 1

The real person of contention is not the national author who has lambasted an ethnic culture but the writer who uses positive images of ethnic realities in his work to advance his personal career or the cause of the nation he or she belongs to.

The national writer who uses positive elements of ethnic culture in his or her work is the person we have to watch out for. It is this writer who will step into the arena when the "real stuff" is unavailable for exploitation. Concerns for appropriation of voice should normally appear at this point but they rarely do; ethnics scarcely possess the means or power to bring such matters to higher legal offices. In extreme cases, many ethnic writers hardly have the means to fight battles on serious copyright infringements.

The Ethnic Writer

1. The Ethnic writer who uses positive elements of his or her culture in his or her work.
2. The Ethnic writer who uses negative elements of his or her culture in his or her work.

3. The Ethnic writer who does not write about his or her culture but uses the elements of his or her culture to alter form.

The Ethnic Writer 1

There are a handful of critics today are who are quick to jump with joy when they catch direct allusions in texts written by ethnic writers that appropriately point to their ethnic background.

No longer does the press expect ethnic writers to boast about their culture, we expect them to open all the secret drawers of their intimate lives in order to reveal their heritage as a backward or counterproductive force.

The ethnic writer who does not overtly speak of things ethnic is abruptly tossed aside as being irrelevant by Comparative Literature Studies, Italianists, as well as Literature Departments. These scholars even prefer negative stereotypes on culture to positive complexities. The ethnic writer who speaks in positive terms of his or her ethnic culture is somewhat problematic. Critics face positive ethnic writers with some dread: What does an ethnic writer reveal to the host nation when he or she gloats over the positive aspects of a culture the writer should leave behind?

If it is nostalgia that is being promoted, then the critic readily dismisses the dubiousness lack of professionalism of the work. There can be no value in works produced by men and women who feel nostalgia for a land that is not their present home.

If a work is too exultant about the past, critics do not hesitate in pointing their fingers to the door out of the nation. "If the land you left behind is so fine, what are you doing here? Go back home."

This sort of insolence is precisely the reason why many ethnic writers end up retreating into a fantasy world that is neither here nor there. Pasquale Verdicchio claims: "Can we go 'home' again? Yes, however we can't stay."

Many ethnic writers today find themselves in this *in bilico* state, balancing between a fantastic world of confusing identities and lost paradises and a real world that has shut its door to them.

These ethnic writers should be of great concern to ethnic communities all over the world; these orphans live their lives in illusions and delusions which translate into loneliness and loss of hope.

The national media and national cultures care little for these heroic voices in the desert, at the margins of everything. They are aware that these writers serve no purpose for the nation they inhabit, nor for the nation they left behind; these writers don't even have much to offer to other writers, so caught up are they in their ivory towers of rediscovered identities that are as difficult to appreciate as they are to understand. Confusion in the end leads to more confusion, and nothing will come from nothing.

The Ethnic Writer 2

The national media (and all its contraptions) has its eyes on one type of ethnic writer: the one who tarnishes his or her culture. It is this ethnic writer that the adopted nation wants to attract to its flock.

Here is a person who has lost all respect for whom she or he is; the nation knows that by recompensing this self-hating writer with fame and money, it will have converted the lost sheep to its nationalist cause.

This is the sort of writer who makes the headlines, who reaps the glory most young writers expect when they publish their works.

The only accepted ethnic writer is the one who has relinquished his or her identity and is ready to embrace a new culture. And if there is no Ethnic Writer 2 available, we move along and ask Nationalist Writer 1 to do the work.

The Ethnic Writer 3

The ethnic writer who works forms to describe who he or she is, who invents an identity that shall never attract the attention of the nation is the least desirable kind of writer. Here is the scientist of poetry, here is where we find the artist working in a laboratory searching for the proper alchemy that will change collective unconsciousness into individual *imaginaire,* that will change individual unconsciousness into collective consciousness.

The ethnic writer who speaks highly for what he or she has left behind can only be a nuisance and an embarrassment to the rest of the nation. What is there to say about the ethnic writer who not only speaks cautiously about all origins but also denies art its easiness of expression? Why is creativity all of a sudden like an undiscovered environment that needs to be analyzed and controlled?

So far most literary critics have interminably concentrated on questions of content and disregarded formal analysis when it comes to the works of ethnics. Formal experimentation has always been viewed as suspicious by the power elite, and so wherever a woman and a ethnic writer begin to delve into such Faustian matters of art the critics' apprehension only doubles in intensity.

Content alone rarely unveils the identity of a writer. Content can be easily copied and more often than not is most fruitfully manipulated by talented writers who neither care to identify themselves to the public, nor want to be identified as belonging to any one group. This sort of appropriation of voice eventually smothers other writers who are searching to enrich a collective consciousness.

Many writers demand, and rightly so, that they be exempt from allegiance to political party, race, religion, and ethnic groups. Few writers ever attain such a praise-worthy social status. To be a beacon for all humankind is the unexpressed goal of many artists, but a goal that is seldom attained.

When scholars and critics decide to label writers and slide these writers' works into certain slots, it is not to diminish the uniqueness of the writer. Most do so to facilitate understanding of the works in question.

Classification of writers is an inescapable side-effect of criticism. When one speaks of a particular tradition to explain a work, it is not to belittle the work's singular elements. It is precisely because the work is so uncommon and exceptional that it needs to be grounded in a more familiar foundation. Once elements of commonness are detected, then we can begin to grasp the degree of conformity or non-conformity to the models established by the writers and works which preceded the writer and work under study.

The convention has been to use national culture as point of reference and language as the common denominator to define tradition. With the abandonment of a national culture as a unifying trait, will language alone suffice to interpret artistic lineage? This is a matter for debate; we believe it won't.

Writers may take one of ten possible positions: the Nationalist, the Exile, the Transmuter, the Nostalgic, the Hermit, the Palatine, the Tinsel, the Ethnic, the Ultra-Nationalist, and the Dreamer. In parenthesis we have used the terms *here* and *there* in ten different combinations, the *here* representing the present time and the immediate geographical situation of the single writer and the *there* representing the atemporal and non-geographical presence of the writer. Each separate term may also be replaced by the name of a country (for example, here = America; there = Italy); this simple exercise will make it easier to follow our reasoning.

Our obstinate use of categories here is purely analytical. They are signposts meant to indicate paths that draw people to some sort of understanding of what superior role literature and cultural artifacts play in our modern and fragmented society.

1. The Nationalist (Here/Here)

This writer belongs to the tradition of the country he or she is living in. This writer adopts, totally, whatever tradition is alive in the country he or she is presently living in.

2. The Exile (Here/There)

This writer belongs to a tradition initiated in his or her country of origin which the writer had to leave for personal or political reasons. What is important to note is that the physical move has not in appearance displaced the writer in a spiritual, cultural, or economic way. Though living abroad, the Exile continues to publish and be active in the country of his or her origin.

The following are fine examples of writers in exile, or who have emigrated: Anne Hébert continued to be a Quebecois writer even though she had been living in France for over thirty years. Gore Vidal continues to be an American writer even though he has been living in Italy for decades.

3. The Transmuter (There/Here)

This writer sheds the tradition of his or her origins and adheres totally to the tradition rising from his or her country of adoption.

In this group we find writers who let go of their origins and embrace a new language and tradition.

Famous Transmuters are Joseph Conrad and Milan Kundera.

4. The Nostalgic (There/There)

This writer wants desperately to belong to a tradition of the past, of his or her land of origin. In fact, the Nostalgic's position is not considered as being part of any official culture; neither of the country left behind, nor of the country he or she lives in.

This writer uses a language of the native country hoping that his or her work will be acknowledged by the culture of the motherland, distancing himself or herself from the country he or she lives in. Unfortunately, neither the motherland, nor the adopted country cares for this kind of writer since his or her allegiances lie only with himself or herself. There can be no selfishness when it comes to questions of culture.

5. The Hermit (Here/There^Here)

This writer belongs to a tradition associated with a language that is not part of the official tradition of the "natural" environment in which his or her work is produced.

This group of writers consists mostly of disinterested men and women who do not care to have the privileges of the Exiles nor the dreamy otherness of the Nostalgics; the Hermit works alone using the language of another country either for his own pleasure or politics. The main point here is that the Hermit does not care to be accepted by any country. The language and tradition chosen by the writer do not confer any sort of legit-imization, neither from the official tradition of the country the writer is living in, nor from the official tradition of the country of origin (which the Exile receives). Unlike the Nostalgics, who claim rights from their abandoned territory and who live in nowhere land, with an eye always to the country he or she left behind, the Hermit claims one territory, that of the imagination.

6. The Palatine (Here/There*There*)

This writer belongs to no group. This writer refuses to give his or her allegiance to tradition, language, or nation. This writer cares neither for traditions, languages, nor countries; nor does he or she want to be part of any tradition, language, and country. Typically this writer invents his or her own tradition, language, and country.

Few in number, the Palatines are solitary geniuses who glow like literary gods. James Joyce, Claude Gauvreau and Patrick Straram are three Palatines that come to mind.

7. The Tinsel (There/Here*Here*)

This writer rebukes whatever one tradition has given him and advances the nationalist policies of the adopted country's tradition. Usually this writer speaks disparagingly of his or her original culture in order to gain prestige in another culture. The *there* was bad, therefore the *here* is best. The point of interest with Tinsels is how they are able to turn criticism from members of their past cultures to their advantage: they cunningly magnetize to themselves the ultimate glorious compliment of being a persecuted writer, a persecution which only further intensifies the Tinsel's claim of being born into a bad culture.

8. The Ethnic (There/Here^{There})

This writer strives for a supra-linguistic, nation-free tradition. The presence of the double elsewhere, the *there* as the power of two, brings the Ethnic close to the Palatine. But there are major differences between the Palatine and the Ethnic.

The Palatine begins with a territorialized national culture and goes off towards something else; the Ethnic does not have a territorialized national culture. Because the Palatine needs to free himself or herself of the weight of territory, the Palatine aims for individualism.

The Ethnic never had a territory to begin with and was a solitary writer; the target is therefore something less individualistic, more collective. The Ethnic wishes to connect with the other solitary writers of the world.

The Palatine has a language he or she wants to get rid of or destroy; the Ethnic has no language and never will. The Palatine's universality is individualistic; the Ethnic's collective.

The two other possible positions, the Ultra-Nationalist (*Here/Here^{Here}*) and the Dreamer (*There/There^{There}*), do not need further explanation.

The struggle for collective universalism is the first criterion for admissibility into the Ethnic group. What I call *Italic* is a subgroup of the Ethnic. It is our personal way of freeing our work from nationalistic prisons which many scholarly discourses on Italian-this, Italian-that have locked writers into. Critics should be wary of the way they approach the analysis of works by minority writers. Not all writers play the same role, for not all writers lead in the same direction. A similar word frequently signifies two different things in any two writers. Never take the vocabulary of writers for granted.

Each writer has preferences and each person takes decisions in one or another direction. It is the critic's job to see how these preferences and decisions affect the nature of the work. One must decipher the equations of ideas and images created by writers, not just underscore the fact that one person has ten percent of this or that sort of blood. Each equation leads to proposed solutions; what solutions do authors offer their society?

Membership into a cultural community must be *voluntary, not automatic.* The choice to be or not to be part of anything is a right. Literature must be the product of democracy, not cultural dictatorship. It is this freedom of choice that will lead us into the forum of the untiring study of culture.

Without this decision have we, as critics, the right to consider certain writers Italics (even though they have, to be vulgar about it, Italian blood), if they go about ravaging the culture in the name of another culture, if the writers themselves repeatedly remind us that they no longer are Italians?

No use in continuing the discussion of a particular work of a writer if the author systematically refuses to belong to the group. It would be unfair to this writer's freedom of choice – this choice which should remain at all times the one and only valid *sine qua non*. If there is no freedom of choice, there can be no further discussion on the issue. Membership in any other group is not meant to be wrought with honors or privileges. Membership is free of charge, so to say, and cannot bring about rewards simply because one is a member of a group. Any writer is, first and foremost, master of his or her own domain.

Rooting for the Opposite Team

In a few weeks I will be going to Italy for the *n*th time with the hope of convincing Italian publishers to translate just one of the many Italian-Canadian authored books into Italian. I have been trying in vain for twenty years. Italian publishers are closed to things that are not moneymakers. That, of course, excludes most great novels of the century. Greatness does not necessary imply a money making venture.

The other day I read in *La Repubblica* how it took over fifteen years to translate into Italian a Nobel Prize winner in literature. I wasn't shocked one bit. And it came as no surprise when I read in *Tandem* that Italians came in last as far as reading was concerned. This apathy to literature translates itself, abroad, into foreigners' apathy to much of what is done in Italy today. Italy is nice only as a monument of the past.

Most Italian authors translated into English rarely get reviewed or even noticed on this continent. This indifference to Italian literature is disturbing, I admit, but when compared to the indifference Italian North American authors receive in Italy, one can't help but sigh that divine destiny is acting out its role.

One would imagine that there would be great interest in the literature that Italy has produced this century, but there isn't. Dario Fo, who recently won the Nobel Prize, had never been translated into English. And it is the same story the other way round. John Fante, the great Italian-American writer, has only recently been translated into Italian. He had been translated by the French over twenty-five years ago, and the Dutch made two films based on his novels over a decade ago. Okay, Italians are slow. But this is ridiculous.

What is more astonishing is to hear Italians baffled by the reasons why Fante, who is published by a small press in California, should now be a bestseller in Italy. Little does Italy realize how much it has to gain in translating as much as it can. Translation will make its culture progress.

It's surprising that Italians are not given the chance to read what Italians abroad have been doing this past century. It might help them with their recent immigration problems.

The other day I read somewhere that Italy has become suddenly fascinated by the Irish immigration experience in Canada. It is true that the Irish diaspora can be appealing to the stranger, but why should Italy suddenly lend a hand to the Irish when it never showed the least interest in what its cousins abroad were living? I don't think that this silencing is innocent. It is purely financial, and this is a pity, since finance should be giving a hand to culture.

Italians are bicephalous: one head for the bank book, the other for calculating the idiosyncratic pleasures this bank book can procure. Where is the heart? No wonder there are so many Italian joining religious sects.

Italians are no different here. According to Stats

Canada, Italians rank up there with the rich, yet hit rock bottom when it comes to education.

Perhaps all of this bickering makes me sound a bit anti-Italian. I assure you, I am not. It is just that I realize that I'm wasting my time going to Italy for cultural purposes.

The night before boarding the plane I will ask myself why is it that I continue to want to be an Italian? Why not simply change my name, dye my hair, and root for the opposing team?

Failure

The Saturday paper talks about the war a country has declared on one of its ethnic communities.

I am listening to "Blues for Pablo" by Miles Davis, an artist who could not walk through the front door of the establishments he played at. Always through the back door.

The bread I am eating is giving me blisters in my mouth: the company that bakes this bread is using more than one hundred percent whole wheat. What crap are they adding to it?

The cigarette that I light up contains arsenic and carbon dioxide and over one thousand chemicals that are not good for my health. If I want to live a little longer, I should quit smoking.

These sentences are no different than the sentences I first wrote in 1967, in a brand new notebook where I scribbled my thoughts about a world that frankly left me dumbfounded. I was young, in love, and that young love tormented me, which made me want to scream against all forms of social injustice.

Writing entails a need for analysis, and as feeble as this analysis might be, it is my way of coming to grips with the world of politics in general and the culture that has made me the person I am.

I love reading the obscure verses of formalist poets, and yet when I close the book I feel that these texts leave me with the impression that they are the product of some aristocratic past-time. An experience, bordering on the sexual, which excludes the Other.

The pleasure is valuable, I appreciate that, yet my enthusiasm is lukewarm. Not so much because of the private pleasures found therein, as much as the fact that the poetry that results seems to me somewhat bland.

Formalism, to use a fashionable term, leaves me cold. Be it French-language formalism (deconstruction of syntax and meaning) or English-language and Italian-language formalism (a revival of neo-classicism), they appear to be the expressions of literature in decadence – the knowledge of a specific cultural group attaining its zenith and from there on rolling its way down – and the crisis of a particular intelligentsia. I might be wrong. It is a gut feeling.

The twilight of one period in history necessarily pulls out the dawn of a new period of history.

The writer has three roads to choose from: 1. he can hang onto waning literary tastes; 2. he can subvert these tastes in decadence and use them as seed for new vegetation; 3. or, if he is unable to follow neither of these paths, he can invent his own voice, working alone, at the periphery of literature and society.

Many modern writers fit into the first category. They bathe in the waters of the glorious past, at times using the past technical achievements with irony, yelling so loud as to tear language apart, bombarding it to the maximum, until it finally collapses, lifeless.

This literary activity bores me. Of course, I am the first one to praise its linguistic games and somersaults but, at the end of the day, all this fooling around gets on my nerves. And I am by no means a conservative.

The poets of the second category are undoubtedly more fascinating. They point to new horizons, indicating the way to dig and where to find markers for tomorrow. Obsession does not make them turn their heads to the past for answers, for they know that they are the period at the end of the sentence.

Counter to popular belief, Nicole Brossard only skimmed the surface of the formalist movement of the first category. She rather rapidly dove into invention. On the one hand, she discovered feminist writing; on the other hand, she became essentially a writer of the third category. This is why Nicole Brossard has become an unforgettable voice in contemporary literature. She is not alone, manifestly. She works outside the genre system, and has candidly done what had to be done to uproot the monuments of the past and plant them on unknown territory.

The great writers of the third category have a writing so personalized that it is as individual as their fingerprints. They distinguish themselves from writers of the second category by the disregard they show for the past and future. Their writing is atemporal, without geography, at the limits of language, belonging to no particular political party, wagering against all odds. Léo Ferré sings their praise more beautifully than I ever can. All I can say is that they are squirrels, gnawing here and there on shells that eventually crack open to reveal creative delights.

Barry Callaghan is the most underrated writer in this country. His nib splits open on every word, his sentences transform table talk into mythological apostrophes. He writes in English, but his forms are continental. His poetry is barrelhouse speeches only silver-tongued orators can utter. His short stories, the playground for the lucky shot, should be called *récits*; exaggeration is so predominant that fiction sounds like age-old wisdom. Frankness never confirms literalism; it deceives as much as trickery. Critics stand in awe before such masterful equivocalness that many attack him for not respecting reality. Writers of the third category know that their real world is coming to an end. Barry Callaghan, one could say, is the last English-language writer of Canada.

Patrick Straram was no formalist. Nor was he a precursor of a new movement. He walked alone on a path he had paved for himself. He was one of a kind in French-language literature. Just as was Claude Gauvreau. So was James Joyce in his non-language (or ultra-language) monster of a work, *Finnegans Wake*.

To mention these names unsettles the mind. We do not like exceptions. We prefer simplicity. What is simplicity, if not the style most writers of the third category often adopt to delude the reader. Simplicity, when it appears, is counterfeit money of the best kind. The great writer is like the albatross, to use a Baudelairean cliché: a bird beautiful to watch flying, but on land its tremendously large wings prevent it from walking. The essential writer is the writer who ruffles the world around him just by being there.

Every writer of every category can become an essential writer. He must first learn to detach himself from his peers and promise transformation. The act is a wager that brings about political and social change. In so doing, the essential writer must at times forsake quality (not that the work itself is intrinsically lacking in quality, the quality is still present), so that his work may appear to lose its price value by market standards.

To speak crookedly, badly. But also to utter bad ideas.

Ezra Pound and Louis-Ferdinand Céline were horribly intolerant towards certain ethnic communities. Notwithstanding such unacceptable hatred, does their work justify ostracism?

The writer of the third category writes his everyday world and, by chronicling this everyday existence, he unravels the terrible secrets kept behind closed doors by the society in which he lives.

The writer's language emerges from the being he is, the accounts he spreads out before us will automatically appear to be political. How can he remain aloof if his style corresponds to the political world he lives in? His being itself is adumbrated in the presentation, less from personal ethnic impropriety (which is a possibility, fortunately or unfortunately), than from the inescapable presence he has committed to existence. His work embraces a frightening solitude.

It is not the quality of solitude that separates the writers of one category from the other, but the work. You cannot approach the work as a pseudo-scientist. Pascal expressed a similar criticism in regard to mathematics: to lock yourself up in an ivory tower will cut you off from the things of the world.

In the first two categories, everyday life is looked upon like a fossil to be studied. The problem is not with this sort of laboratory analysis, but the attitude with which the writer approaches the work. Nowadays, only the latest discoveries are rewarded. But discovery is not *being.* It is only the quality of lens you use to focus on being. Real discoveries demand the critical exploration *of* the work before your eyes, not the praising of the researcher.

We are noticing a growing number of artists, in all fields, for whom art is showbiz. If you read the reviews published in papers and magazines, you could conclude that everyone has become a genius. We have forgotten that what counts is not popular or monetary success, but the process of creativity.

In many ways, we should spend less time on success and more time on failure. At least, there, we would meet a person who took aim at the bull's eye, but missed. I purposely did not say the *aim* was wrong – that would lead to a discussion on the politics of meritology: "Who came up with the target in the first place? Who positioned the target on the wall? Who will compose the jury to adjudicate the results?"

To answer these questions would change the focus of the argument and take us to considerations of respectability. He who dares answer these questions would have to be honest and show everyone the cards in his desk. He who wants to play must play by the rules of the industry of success. Indisputably. And who can do that today? For a game to be taken seriously, it has to be taken seriously by society at large. If a certain section of society refuses to play, then the game becomes compromised and worthless.

Literary awards in Australia do not strike any chord in Germany. An important literary award in Quebec means absolutely nothing to English Canada. Such insularity punctuates the fact that literature is consensually regional. It is not blindly transferable. A translator can translate the work, but not the cultural sources that gave birth to the text (unless the translator is the writer).

Here lies a paradox. Does a thing worthy on the regional level lose its worth once it attempts to become universal? No use replying, since we have chosen to translate only what is successful in one region to another. It's a compromise.

But there are works that are not at all success stories, yet deserve to be translated, transported from one culture to another. Still, we are told that such works cannot be translated because they are too regional, too parochial. The dice are loaded.

Translating "failures" would challenge the whole notion of what is a success back home. Better to silence, therefore, what could create problems. I'm convinced, however, that time will sort things out. On this point, I am an optimist. There will always be a curious adolescent who will open the forgotten boxes in the neighbor's basement.

The less a text is known the more curious I become. There is always something to gain from what is not viewed favorably by critics and the establishment. The writers of the third category are those that the pillars of society wrap in anonymity. They are the solitary men and women whose voices are too dangerously non-conformist. These voices are music to my ears. They are treasure chests brimming with words I need to listen to. They are the sounds that will blossom into an undying imaginary flower.

I do not believe in the literary quarrels as presented to us in our literary journals. What do I care if rhyme or syllables ratify the success of a poem?

Maybe we are not teaching T.S. Eliot as we should at university. Professors of literature are responsible for

ANTONIO D'ALFONSO

the incredible rage that pushes a writer to follow certain mannerisms in order to be successful. Teachers
should not exclude other possibilities. I don't believe
Eliot wanted tradition to be a way of preserving con-
servatism, no matter how conservative he might have
been as a human being.

Tradition is there to be discussed and transcended,
not imitated. How can we begin to grasp the fragmented world we live in, if we tie it up in the straight-
jackets of the Middles Ages? Yes, specialization is great
for laboratories, but not for everyday life.

Bombs start dropping in your kitchen, and you can't be
thinking about how to make them rhyme with you.

If a rhyme happens by chance, okay; but if by
attempting to achieve a cute rhyme you sacrifice the
life of your daughter, then it's better to stutter out of
poetry.

Translation: A Sacrifice

Translating. Can I convey faithfully in another language, the language, syntax, and vision of a poet? Faithfully? Faithful to whom? To what? Translation is a social contract, a marriage between two languages and two peoples.

When a critic condemns a translation, when he doubts the value of a translation, he is in fact refusing to be impressed by poetry. There is no really bad translation; every translation will be off, will fail to replicate the original. What is offered is a work that stands parallel to the original text.

Each translator has a voice that requires that we attentively listen, in order to fully appreciate the work.

Translating entails conveying what happens in one language, linguistically and symbolically, into another language. A poem is not static.

My job is to study the direction in which the words are moving. How do I transpose this fabrication from one poem to another? By cautious maneuvering.

The other evening I assisted at a presentation of *Othello*. It was the first time I had heard Shakespeare performed in French. The experience was disappointing.

When Desdemona died, the audience broke out in laughter. I asked myself why. The spectators were expecting to see the transferral of a universal emotion to a regionalized context. Something the actors and the director and the translator declined to do. They chose to remain faithful to the sixteenth-century syntax and vocabulary. The result was distortion, and we, the audience, reacted to the untruthfulness of the transposition, in spite of the fact that the translation was superb and authentic, and the acting was meticulous. What occurred was that a portion of the emotions belonging to the English people got ensnared before finding its way, deformed, to the French-speaking Quebecois audience. A trap opened, and down slid the veracity of feeling.

In every poet, the voice of the community of origin can be heard. You have to listen carefully but it is there, and that is the voice that must get translated. More than the words, the voice, the tradition, the history of a people are calling out to be authenticated in another reality. In this particular case, the translator might have considered using standard French, colored by what makes the Quebecois the persons they are.

We cannot expect one translation to be suitable for audiences sharing a common language but living in different territories. Every country is entitled to its own translations of foreign works. This performance of *Othello* might have worked for a French-speaking audience in France, but not in Quebec. One could not propose a British translation of a German play to an American audience. There are certain realities that are not shared.

More than imitating magnificently the syntax of the extraordinary phrases by Shakespeare, the translator might have transposed the texts into a standard French being used in Quebec by its modern dramatists. He might have balanced himself, as much as possible,

alongside Shakespeare, instead of adopting the weakened position of a colonized victim.

A translator should never be inferior to the author
being translated. The translator must stand his ground
and be confident, strong, conscious of the weight he is
carrying on his shoulders. Using syntactical inversions
and an antiquated vocabulary become overpowering
ornaments for modern ears.

The translator should be aware of what must be
achieved at a precise moment. Translations should be
modern re-readings of what was accomplished.

Translation calls for a sacrifice of the imagination.
Voluntary destruction and gracious surrendering are
indispensable if one wishes to produce a literary transposition worthy of the original text.

The Quest for Authenticity
(Or the Other Side of the Anti-passion)

Interview with Denise Brassard

Between Fiction and Reality

Denise Brassard: *You have written so much about yourself that one could say that your writing is autobiographical. It is difficult to separate the person from the writer.*

Antonio D'Alfonso: You believe that my writing is autobiographical. It's not true.

D. B.: *Let's say that it is like a self-portrait. Do you consider yourself a writer who creates self-portraits?*

A.D.: What you are saying is interesting. All that I write is invention. I use narrators. People who know me well never feel as though I am writing about them. I take what I can from reality and quickly alter its parameters so as not to hurt my family and friends.

D.B.: *Of course. Whatever we write is to a large degree invention. To make a portrait of someone or a self-portrait you need various points of view. You mention this in a moving text, "Porte tournante," in* Comment ça se passe: *"Je suis le cinabre d'où l'on tire le mercure que les étameurs coulent derrière vos glaces. Je suis le miroir qui réfléchit ce qui n'a pas de reflet." ("I am mercury extracted from cinnabar, which smiths use to silver the backs of your mirrors. I am the mirror reflecting that which has no reflection" – translated by Jonathan Kaplansky.) This passage illustrates how sensitive you are to point of view. This is part of your personal quest for identity.*

A.D.: Yes, I strive for this autobiographical tone. Yet I want to allow myself a few lies. In *Comment ça se passe* one finds, nevertheless, two real characters. Lorraine and Hélène exist in real life. A boyhood friend who read the book said to me one day: "I didn't know that you felt like that about Hélène." I decided on the spot that I would never again call people by their real names. I probably did so in the first place because I wanted to open myself up totally to my readers.

D.B.: *You often dedicate your texts to friends and acquaintances. You either talk directly to them or else you quote them. The poem for Daniel Sloate comes to mind, and the one to Pasquale Verdicchio.*

A.D.: Yes, it is as if I were sending them a letter. My texts are letters to friends, writers, or some person I just met. A text is like a matting into which I weave elements from reality. My friends do complain, though, that I never write truthfully about my real life, nor do I ever say what I think of the world. A dedication is like a kiss I give a friend. It is my way of winking and saying, Thank you.

D.B.: *Among these people, some stand out like emblems: Gaston Miron and Patrick Straram, in particular, who appear in many of your texts. In one poem in* Comment ça se passe, *you speak about them in very concrete terms.* "Toronto la nuit ressemble à Montréal / quand je marchais seul après avoir jasé avec Straram ou Miron. / Seulement ils ne sont plus là, ici, à mes côtés, pour m'accompagner / comme Virgile accompagnait Dante à travers sa nuit." *(Toronto at night looks like Montreal / when I come back home alone, after having talked with Straram or Miron. /*

They are no longer there, here, beside me / as Virgil went with Dante when he walked through his night.") One gets the impression that these men represent more than just a literary tradition. They appear to be people you loved dearly.

A.D.: Gaston Miron helped me. He was a spiritual father to me. I do not say this because, now that he is dead, it is fashionable to speak about Miron. I sent him my first poetry book in 1973 and, from that moment, we spent time together. He showed up at Guernica's first book launching in 1979. It did not matter that the books being launched were in English. He came to visit me, years later, in Italy. We spoke about everything, and soon we became quite close. Miron taught me how to become a publisher.

D.B.: *How did he react when he found out you were moving to Ontario?*

A.D.: He was the only person (with Janou Saint-Denis) to call me up and ask me to stay. When I explained my reasons for leaving, he understood. Still, he did not want me to go.

D.B.: *What about Patrick Straram?*

A.D.: I learned about Patrick Straram from my reading of Philippe Haeck. It must have been in 1974 or 1976, I don't recall. I bought one of his books, *Questionnement socratique,* which changed my life. It is one of the few books that left an indelible imprint on my spirit.

D.B.: *Did you ever meet him?*

A.D.: Yes. I was doing my Masters degree at the Université de Montréal and was hired in those days as an assistant-professor at Loyola College, now called

Concordia University. Every Friday evening – or it could have been every night – I don't remember, I saw Patrick at the Cinémathèque run by Serge Losique. Every night, one could see Patrick sitting, first row center, in the third seat on the left, dressed like a native American (he called himself Le bison ravi), a beautiful woman to his side. He was younger then, alcohol had not yet ravaged him as it did by the end of his short life (he died at fifty-two). People don't agree with me, but I remember him as having a strong body.

D.B.: *He was quite charismatic. Many considered him a guru of sorts. They listened to what he had to say, drinking his every word, never truly talking to him. This is what filmmaker Serge Gagné confided in me some time ago.*

A.D.: What can I say? I went right up to him and we became close. I translated one of his poems once for a Montreal magazine. Later, when the editorial committee of *Vice Versa* turned his texts down, I quit the magazine I had helped found. We could not turn down a text by Straram. We shouldn't have. I loved Patrick. His writing style was unique. His poems read like a book of quotations, or an essay, or even a film. He had a truly brilliant mind; he was a true beacon, in the Baudelairean sense of the word. More so than Miron, whom I loved as a human being and publisher and poet – that goes without saying. For some reason, it was Straram's texts that really called out to me. He came from a wealthy Parisian family. He was a Protestant. He was very mathematical in his creativity. He wrote like he was. His mathematical-like texts bordered on what could not be contained. If you read his writings, you will see all of this fire and restraint working hand in hand. His non-linearity brought you to another level of significance. He influenced me in many ways. After reading Straram, I threw the verse form out of the window.

Historian of His Own Life

D.B.: *If your writing is not autobiographical, you nevertheless are concerned with creating a history for yourself and with writing the story of this personal history, even if you have to invent it. The first part of* L'Apostrophe qui me scinde *has as title:* Historian of His Own Life. *You say that it is your job as poet to invent history. What strikes me in particular about these texts is the presence of mythical characters. They are present in every text. Especially Circe and Antigone, who come out as antinomic figures. Circe is a stop in your journey, the impossibility of moving ahead. She represents death. Antigone is . . .*

A.D.: Resistance.

D.B.: *In* L'Apostrophe qui me scinde *something quite interesting happens. One finds mannerisms in your writing that are quite surprising, which clash with the texts that you will write later on. You continuously play with mythical figures, as though we were being asked to assist at the dismantling of statues and monuments. In fact, in* Comment ça se passe, *these figures no longer appear. They are . . .*

A.D.: Dead.

D.B.: *. . . almost totally absent. Simultaneously, in your books, you have a very ambiguous relationship with death. The dead do not want to die. They come to haunt the living. I believe there is a correlation to establish between Circe and* *how death is reified, "statufied." And yet we see a link to what you say about the New Baroque, as defined by you. The New Baroque is both a way to bridge yourself to the past and a way to break away from it. Much like the manner you use myth. You explore the past in detail, allowing mythology to run through you. You play with geography and mythological figures and then tear everything down in order to move forward.*

A.D.: The first book I published in 1973 was inspired by an Inuit myth. I have always gone back to the past to find answers. I did it for my short films, and I do it in this script I wrote with actress Jennifer Dale. I was influenced by Cocteau. I want to do what he did. I think I achieve it in my novel, *Avril ou l'anti-passion (Fabrizio's Passion)*. I am indebted to Cocteau and Pasolini. Both have played a fundamental role in my intellectual development.

Poetry and Translation: Making Life Go in a Certain Direction

D.B. *In the last section of* L'Apostrophe qui me scinde, *you clearly distinguish poetry and prose. That text reads like an* ars poetica. *You say that prose is no less poetic than poetry, but it is easier to translate. You also admit that you dream in Italian and that you spend a lot of time translating. Furthermore, in your books, you sometimes include texts that have been translated. At times, you mention a translator, at times you say nothing about the translation. Is this due to the fact that you write poetic prose more often than verse?*

A.D.: I wanted to practice a genre that is non–existent in English, the *récit,* where language is stripped of artifice, purged, and where fat is trimmed to a minimum. In my opinion, the *récit* is the greatest of all literary forms. Nothing happens in a *récit* and yet syntax leads you to another level of significance, into the personal level. Every aspect of the *récit* is personalized. You don't find that in English literature. I discovered what could be done with the *récit* while I was translating Philippe Haeck's prose poetry, another writer who also plays an important role in my writing. That is when I told myself: "I love prose, poetic prose." *The Other Shore* was originally written in verse. But I changed all of that and kept only a handful of poems in verse form.

D.B.: *Were you reacting to English-language culture?*

A.D.: No, since one faces similar obstacles in French. We find certain attitudes in every culture. In England, in the U.S.A., in Italy, most writers of my generation have gone back to classical forms: rhyming schemes, neo-classical writing. I did not want to do that, nor did I want to write like Ginsbger, Kerouac, or Ferlinghetti. I did not want to imitate what had been done by the Beat generation: automatist writing of sorts. What I do not appreciate about English-language writing is that poets use rhyme and structured versification to literally imitate prosaic narrative. Between neo-classical forms and automatist writing, there is an unexplored territory. This is why I chose to write a very structured poetic prose.

D.B.: *Is this sort of writing easy to translate because it is in prose? That's what you claim in the text.*

A.D:. Yes, I allow myself the freedom to transpose

certain syntactical details in ways that best express what is important: vision.

D.B.: *Is this possible because you don't have to deal with structured verse?*

A.D.: Of course. The French use hexameters. Whether French-language writers compose hexameters consciously or not is irrelevant. It is always there in the background. Hexameters don't work in English. English-language writers have this life-long obsession about translating Dante in verse. Everyone takes a crack at it. There are about fifteen translations of Dante's *Divine Comedy* on the market today. It's ridiculous. I gave up trying to read these translations and went out to buy a prose translation of that masterpiece. Why even try to translate what is impossible to translate? Not the meanings, the verses. In Italian, rhyming is super easy. Every word ends in *o* or *a*. If it ends with a consonant it is usually because they dropped the vowel at the end of the word. Since every word has a vowel, all that a writer needs to do is basically concentrate on the meter. Translating an Italian verse of five unstressed syllables into English, a language which, culturally speaking, has imposed five stressed syllables, or into French, which works in twelve feet, would produce something totally different, even if the rhyme scheme were respected. The exercise is senseless. Better to translate a lot of the stuff into straight prose. I read Virgil in prose. It was better than any of the verse translations I ever read of the works of this great poet.

D.B.: *It is true that most epic poetry in French has been*

translated for the modern reader into prose. Translators must have realized that it was just a waste of time to do otherwise.

A.D.: Well, it does offer you some kind of pleasure, in the Barthean sense of the term. I sometimes fidget with translating texts of the past. It is fun, but they will never read like Dante. I prefer reading a good prose piece, instead of this stuff in verse that contains seventy-five footnotes on every page, as is usually the case with such translations. At one point, I found myself reading the footnotes instead of the poem. Many readers do. They don't read Dante anymore. They are reading the translator's explicative notes at the bottom of the pages. Forget it. Let me read the past in prose.

D.B.: *When you translate, and I am thinking of your translation of Pasquale Verdicchio's selected poems,* Le paysage qui bouge, *didn't you take too many liberties? I understand that translating poetry requires a degree of adaptation. One has to appropriate the text, still in* Le paysage qui bouge *I noticed that you took some incredible liberties that changed the meaning of the poems. I told myself, luckily there is the original text on the facing page which enables me to compare the two texts. I was able to appreciate the variations. It was like reading Antonio D'Alfonso's explanation about how one should read Verdicchio. In the end, one is sitting in front of two totally different texts.*

A.D.: I did ask the publisher not to include the original texts. I am not in favor of bilingual editions. They are good for university professors who need some excitement.

D.B.: *In your case, one could ask if it is a translation at all.*

A.D.: Of course it is. It is my translation of a friend's

poetry. I took certain liberties when it came to the meaning of certain verses, but I am entitled to do so since I know the author personally. I could ask him for help. At times, though, the meaning was so equivocal that I had to decide on one of two possible meanings. Consider the title: *Moving Landscape.* What does it mean? It does not necessarily mean that the landscape is moving. It could also mean that the landscape is an emotional experience: the landscape moves you.

D.B.: *Granted. I do not question the choices you had to make, which surely took some time to make. You have to distinguish between editorial decisions and creative liberties. I am thinking about those texts where you added what did not even appear in the original.*

A.D.: A critic made a similar criticism about my translation. He was questioning the work on another level, but you are both saying the same thing which is that I have changed the text. When Pasquale reads his poems in public, he is constantly adding lines to his poems. It is those modified poems that I decided to translate. Yes, I did change a line or two, but this is what he himself does to them. And since I know so many of his poems by heart, I did on paper what he does aloud. The real gamble I took was that I chose to latinize the musicality of his poems. I did something similar with Philippe Haeck's poems. You must realize that Pasquale Verdicchio is someone who lives in Italian. He sometimes chooses to purposely make errors in his English texts. He stumbles everywhere, and I am sure he does this intentionally. He wants to make mistakes. The problem is that often these mistakes are glorious; other times, not so. It is in the latter instances that I decided to soften the fall, by trying to find what would work best in French. I could have translated his poems literally, but we would not be here discussing his work. I jokingly say that French is a racist language used by free people and that English is a free language used by racists. I knew who the readers of this translation would be: Quebecois friends. There are many English-language Canadian writers who are Quebecois in spirit. The fact they write in English is of no importance. This was the point of the project. I translated Pasquale Verdicchio as though he were a French-language poet.

D.B.: *Your views of poetry are romantic. Almost essentialist. That's surprising coming from you. Your attempts at defining poetry – like you do in the closing text of* L'Apostrophe qui me scinde *– reveals a polarity: at one pole, you suggest a mechanistic view of poetry, poetry as construction, what comes out of hard work; at the opposite pole, you present poetry as an essence. In fact, you define the poetic (which you distinguish from poetry) as an essence. What you say is a little confusing. Is essence a source or the accomplishment? Reading you I hear Hölderin, Heidegger . . .*

A.D.: I was thinking of Sartre.

D.B.: *There, essence is what follows the making of a poem.*

A.D.: It's not true that it comes after.

D.B.: *Isn't that what Sartre would say?*

A.D.: What I am saying in that text, if I remember correctly, is that I could never translate the Quebecois poetic. The poetic that gives birth to the sort of poetry being written in Quebec, except for the odd production, is unique. Nor would I be able to translate the Italian poetic. The poetic is what emerges from a cultural community, what can be produced with very precise social parameters. This is what I designate as being *essential*. I use the term in the way that Barthes used *connotation* and *denotation*. What he was saying was that connotation is not situated at a higher level than denotation. If anything, perhaps denotation is the highest of levels. This is what I refer to when I speak of the essential.

D.B.: *That reminds me of Goethe saying that the universal is found in small things. Rilke espoused the same idea. And I personally agree. What strikes me about your poetry is to what extent it is intimate. You bring something very personal to people. You expose yourself: you undress yourself, you are fragile, you are never frightened to show your weaknesses or imperfections. You accept it all with lucidity and benevolence. It is a kind of humility that speaks louder than concepts. To come back to translation, if I understand correctly, the poetic is found both in the writing and in the reading. In other words, Gaston Miron translated into Italian could awaken, and participate in, the Italian poetic world, for reasons that would be totally foreign to the Quebecois.*

A.D.: That is the wager. T.S. Eliot said something similar, but in different terms, when he admitted that this experience would happen only with minor poets. A great poet of one culture becomes a minor poet in a second culture; whereas a minor poet, once translated, could very well become a major poet.

D.B.: *Is this due to the fact that a minor poet is not as difficult to translate?*

A.D.: Not really. In the minor poet, we run into a

gamut of mistakes, and it is in those mistakes, I believe, that greatness lies dormant. You don't find it in perfection. A perfect jewel is inevitably unique. For the English, the greatest French poet is not Baudelaire, Rimbaud, Lautréamont, or Éluard; it is Laforgue. The greatest American poet for the French is Poe, who is often not even mentioned as being a poet at all. He is mostly known for his prose works.

D.B.: *Surely, this is because Baudelaire translated him.*

A.D.: Perhaps. Eliot explains this phenomenon in one of his essays. Why is it that the French got so enamored by someone many consider a not-so-fine-poet? Baudelaire, Mallarmé, and Valéry all wrote on Poe. What did these writers see in Poe? Eliot supposes that they were fascinated by Poe's errors. Poe never finished his poems. This was exactly what intrigued Valéry, who saw something essential in Poe's unfinished works. He loved Poe a great deal. For Baudelaire, there was that expression of evil which he associated with the fall of capitalism. In the great American writers, there is nothing of this. In Robert Frost, who is for many the quintessential American poet, the poems are extremely refined. Exactly what the French find uninteresting. All of this talk of failure gave meaning to my own life. Not being a major writer, being more or less a failure myself, I know that my books could very well work in different cultures. What meaning has this realization given to my job as editor? I decided that I would publish minor writers from other cultures. I have succeeded there. It's still a formidable gamble. I might one day wake up and realize that my life has been a failure.

D.B.: *There is a sentence in your latest book that tells us how much your writing has changed. It is telling of what readers feel when they read you.* "Je n'ai plus peur d'écrire comme je parle." *("I'm no longer scared of writing like I talk.") There is an aesthetic bias for realism in this book. You use everyday language and at the same time you have gone back to using verse. I wonder what could have provoked such a transformation. Has this change altered your view of poetry?*

A.D.: The change occurred, like I hinted at previously, with my reading of the neo-classical stuff that is being written by many poets of my generation. The alternative to this returning to the past is not deconstruction. Quebecois poets of the 1970s did that already. I could never write like that. So I had to find my solution elsewhere. I started by reading poetry from different parts of the world. And then, a few years ago, I went to a performance of Jacques Prévert's poetry. I always liked Prévert; his simplicity is never an insult to poetry. He was courageous to write the poems he did when the Surrealists were around. I re-listened to what Léo Ferré and Jean Ferrat did with the poems by Aragon. Again I was quite taken by the simplicity of his verses. This simplicity seemed quite appropriate for the expression of my views on politics. No, I do not write for myself, and yes, I write to transform society. So the main question that needed to be answered was: "How do I write on complex matters without being complex and being free of moralistic garbage?" The answer was obvious, but it had never presented itself to me in this manner before: description. To describe people: that was something that I was never really good at. If I got interested in the writing of film scripts, it was precisely because each scene could be read like a sonnet. And so when I stopped trying to make films, I turned to poetry. The poems in *Comment ça se passe (Getting on with Politics)* came to me as scenes of a film. It was my intention that my poems be read like scenes of a film.

D.B.: *I am shocked by what you are saying. I think you are excellent in the art of portraying people. The moment you let go of the mythological figures you started to assemble a true family photo album. Your images no longer portray idyllic or idealized people; you now talk about ordinary people, your family and relatives. To read* Comment ça se passe *is like fingering through a photo album where we find the occasional self-portrait, which acts like a figure of the double, a recurrent theme in all of your books. You have put distance between yourself and reality and have attained perfect objectivity. I tell myself that this sort of writing is bringing you back to film. This is the poetry of a filmmaker.*

A.D.: This is what I set out to do and will continue to do for some time. I want to describe people, explore their mental states without analyzing their thoughts, without treating people like objects. Not in the way that Francis Ponge did, but by asking myself, for example: "What does a glass of white wine mean?" In a poem, "Premier Amour," I describe what it would be like to wait thirty years before a man makes a woman climax sexually. Imagine: this one husband took thirty years before he was able to make his wife experience orgasm. I wish to write about such magic moments. I no longer need to talk about language; I want to write about the saliva on our tongue.

The Editor: The Urge to Speak

D.B.: *In your book* En Italiques (In Italics) *you spend a lot of time talking about your work as publisher, which seems to be close to your work as translator. You also speak about the challenge you had set for yourself at the beginning, that of bridging different cultures. You rage against the narrow-mindedness of institutions that have no idea where to pigeonhole you, in Quebec as well as Ontario. You also criticize the narrow-mindedness of the reading public. I get the feeling that things have begun to change, at least in Quebec. There is a certain amount of open-mindedness among some publishers and readers. Do you think things are changing? Do you think that you have attained your goals?*

A.D.: No, I have failed. My next book is going to be about failure.

D.B.: *You really believe that you have failed?*

A.D.: Totally.

D.B. *What about this sudden desire for pluralism? Do you think that it is simply an illusion, intellectual posturing?*

A.D.: Pluralism does not exist. Or should I say, it exists, but no one cares for it. Besides, we are too immature to embrace pluralism. Let's take Canada and Quebec. There are Germans and Italians who speak French and English; the Jewish people speak English, French, Yiddish, Hebrew; there are Greeks, Portuguese . . .

Yet second-generation immigrants are incapable of passing on all their post-1970 cultural baggage to following generations. We will have to wait for another generation before this happens. The reason for this is not the fault of these people, but politicians. We have entered the era of anti-difference. Globalization is just another term for warfare. War has a voice, and it is there to silence pluricultural upheavals in every country in the world. To swap nationalism for pluriculturalism means embracing communalism as a political reality. It means that we would have to open up to left-wing programs, whereby what you own you share with your neighbor. It would be the beginning of a new barter system. The president of the U.S.A. and all the multinational companies behind him will have nothing of it.

D.B: *Did you write somewhere that the future of Guernica would be in the U.S.A., not Canada?*

A.D.: I was wrong. The reason I wrote that was because the U.S.A. is not a nation. Quebec is a nation, whether people like to hear it or not. People in Quebec have been living in this one territory and have made it their future. This did not occur in the U.S.A. The Jewish family that lived in New York in 1840 has moved to Chicago or Los Angeles. The Italians of New York have established themselves in Philadelphia or Las Vegas. Ethnic groups spread out constantly in the U.S.A.; they never make a piece of land *their* territory, as the people of Quebec have done. I honestly believed that the U.S.A. would be more promising for a pluricultural future than Canada, which is, after all, limited by laws on bilingualism and biculturalism. There are no such laws in the U.S.A. It is still possible that one day the U.S.A. will become Spanish-speaking. I read somewhere that it almost became German-speaking in the 1800s. Demographics will change the appearance of that country. In Canada, demographics will never be able to exert that sort of cultural pressure, because here laws will make sure that it will not happen.

D.B.: *Would you agree that there is, since 1980, a fictionalized Canadian nationalism being poured all over us? I organized a course on Canadian culture; the group was composed of students who came from all over Canada. For one whole year we asked ourselves what Canadian culture was and if there was such a thing as a single Canadian culture. The answer was "No." There are many Canadian cultures. I noticed that the students who were not from Quebec, when asked by their teachers where they came from (meaning, "Where do your ancestors come from?" instead of "Where were you born?") reacted quite negatively. They automatically adopted a Canadian nationalist stance. They all wished to have this Canadian identity, so much so that they started to argue about the worth of all the cultural symbols they had to invent for this identity. I was surprised by their attitude and fascinated to see that Canada, in wanting to found its identity on territory, had maintained the traces of cultures from abroad. Differences had to be respected. The students embraced their grandparents' cultures, even though all they wished for was to be Canadian.*

A.D.:You are raising a complex issue.We should not forget that English Canada came into being as a resistance to the American Revolution. The people who were against this revolution moved north. They are called the Loyalists. Fulvio Caccia is the expert on this matter, not I. What is clear though is that these Loyalists wanted to preserve the monarchy. Any talk about Canadian identity ultimately leads us to this fact. Criticism of this monarchy is censored in English Canada. For example, if my name is Polynski, and I was born in Regina, say, but now live in Toronto, the center of English-Canadian power, do you believe I stand any chance of making it if I speak against the monarchy? There is a glorification of England in English Canada that is predominant, the great and glorious England. Any author who wants to make it big in this country has to give himself the mission of praising the monarchy. This is obvious to me. We could say that Quebec works in the same way. Only that in Quebec praise for France is never final, since Quebec is the territory to defend. This is why Quebec has never permitted the massive dumping of French products onto its territory.

This creates some strange attitudes. I could spend the rest of my life writing in French, yet people, with a few exceptions, would never consider me a Quebecois writer, even though I was born in Montreal. Likewise, there are very few Quebecois writers who are published outside Quebec who are recognized as Quebecois. There are things one does, and things that one doesn't do. We accept the fact that Anne Hébert was published only in France, as we accept that Jacques Godbout, Marie-Claire Blais, and Suzanne Jacob publish also in France. But there are limits. When it comes to Réjean Ducharme, we all tell ourselves that he had an excuse: he was turned down by five Quebecois publishers. He had no choice but to publish in France. Paradoxically, these writers published abroad are basically the only writers that the Quebecois praise and consider real writers. The others don't really count. Quebec is very much Canadian in this regard. Canadian writers dream of publishing abroad – the English-language writers in England or the U.S.A., and the French-language writers in France. And yet they all want to be the first to write the Great Canadian novel.

D.B.: *Who wants the Great Canadian novel? The Canadians or the Americans?*

A.D.: Canadian writers. But they use American money to strive for it.

D.B.: *You mean that famous Canadian novels are being published by American presses?*

A.D.: Yes, they use their subsidiaries in Toronto. Imagine having, say, Gallimard or Le Seuil in Montreal? Where do you think writers would flock to with their wares? Large presses across the world are slowly buying smaller presses in order to get closer to the new generation of writers. The person with all the cash who spends his time in some fancy hotel simply does not have time to go to all the readings given by younger writers. What he does, instead of buying all the books being published in the country, is to buy smaller presses that are publishing these writers.

D.B.: *What kind of results does this yield? Are there consequences?*

A.D.: What happens is that these large presses end up choosing only one writer in the entire bunch and discarding the rest. What you have today is that many writers are disappearing from the face of the earth. They have no place to publish. This is what I was getting at in *In Italics* when I said that a writer is given one chance to prove himself. If he screws up this one chance, it is all over for him. This is what my next novel is about. Fabrizio is a failure. He realizes that he has never been chosen. This is true of me. It no longer matters if I write two books or fifty books. Miron understood this in his own way. What purpose does it serve if I write seventy-five books when I have not been chosen? My work will never be known. As editor, I told myself that I would publish all these "unchosen" writers in English with the hope of helping Canadian and Quebecois culture.

D.B.: *Do you then believe that the original goals you had when you began Guernica are lost for good?*

A.D.: No, but there is a serious problem if most Canadian writers want to be published by Americans.

D.B.: *Does your classification of the* visiting writer *and the* enduring writer *still make sense?*

A.D.: Writers who publish with Guernica stick around. Only a few have deserted us. I have this sort of conversation with every writer we publish. I try to make him understand that, if I am to spend $10,000 on his career, I would like him to stick around, not because I want to make that money back, I probably never will, but because I like the way he sees the world and the way he writes. I am sure Guernica will find the readers who will appreciate his work.

D.B.: *You say that you will never be considered a Quebecois writer. Yet it was you who began to speak about being Italic, to use your term. It was you who promoted your different identity and pushed it to the fore.*

A.D.: It is not me speaking when I speak. I speak for

my generation, for my cultural community. This too I learned from Miron.

D.B.: *Still, you do use the pronoun* I.

A.D.: For me, *I* equals *we*.

D.B.: *What you are demanding as a "we," the community you are speaking for, is nevertheless otherness.*

A.D.: It is not otherness.

D.B.: *It is pluriethnicity of some kind.*

A.D.: There, yes, I agree with you. But now we are talking about something else all together.

D.B.: *Perhaps. Yet you do mention difference. In fact, you speak quite a lot about difference. The manner in which you develop your concepts is complex. Certain concepts are not clear to me. At times, there is a zone in which everything you say is fuzzy.*

A.D.: The problems arise from the fact that I am using words that others have used before me. I add to these terms a new meaning. I do this on purpose. I approach certain concepts like a writer comes to images. I am not a scholar. I do make sure that I give a definition to all my concepts. The person who reads me knows what words such as *ethnicity, nation, national, pluri-cultural* mean when I say them. When I claim that I am Italian, I never intend to throw this identity in your face like an insult. It is my way of saying that *there,* as André Beaudet would say, is also an elsewhere-here, that this elsewhere is allowed to exist here. What distinguishes you and me is not religion. If I were Jewish, then I would say than I am Jewish and you are not. If my skin color were dark, then I would say I am black and you are not. But I am white, as you are. What makes us different, besides our gender, is not what we eat. This might have been true in the past, but today you probably eat more pasta than I do. Cultures have become so open that it is easy to fall into the trap of stereotypes. I had to learn to use my cultural difference as a value, and this culture has value only if it is glowing with consciousness. Otherwise it is nothing. If I say that I am Italian, Catholic, Quebecois, English-speaking, and you say that you are Irish, French-speaking, Iroquois, then I would be able to deduce that we were from the same place: Quebec. Not from the same nation, but in the same country. This is the reasoning behind my cultural claims. I refuse to speak of nationalism. All I want to do is say that we live in the same country.

Writing the City

D.B.: *The city is rarely mentioned as a singular entity in your books. The city is always described as a network of connections. Your city is presented as a palimpsest where people write. Often you write in one city but talk about a second city. Where you will end up going eventually. I have the impression that a city is never just a city, inasmuch as a city is never alone and is usually compared to another city. I also noticed that you often put dates to your texts and the names of places where these texts were composed, as if you wanted to leave a trace. Do you consider yourself a writer of the city?*

A.D.: Yes. I do not like the country. Dates are traces, yes, I need them. In my next book of poems I have removed all the titles and replaced them by dates. I want to get closer to the diary form. Maybe this is because my memory is falling asleep. I need to leave pebbles behind me.

D.B.: *Talking about his autobiography, Fernand Ouellette said that he felt like Tom Thumb. I had the same sensation as I was reading* Comment ça se passe, *only in reverse. I was reading a diary or an agenda of things to do. In other books, you use parentheses, digressions to say that you have to re-read a certain author or book, or that you are fixing some impossible goal to attain. But in this last book, you set yourself less ambitious tasks and projects. It is as if you were making, more or less, a list of things to get at the grocery store.*

A.D.: You are the second person to say that. Strange. I guess I am becoming simpler in my quest for knowledge. If I write about the city it is because I am scared of traveling. Even though I travel a lot. I always become extremely nervous before I set out on a trip. I always need to know beforehand where I will be staying. Because I suffer from insomnia, I need to know where I will be able to sleep for five or ten minutes in the afternoon. When I write about a city, all I am doing is indicating my landmarks.

D.B.: *Personally, when I am in the country, in front of all that space, I feel closer to myself and become conscious of my limits. I find my center of gravity and who I am. Whereas in the city, because of the presence of so many people and the sudden profusion of urban signs, I feel as though I were spreading myself thin. Intuitively I sense that these contradictions are very much present in your own writings. You have this need for self-affirmation, as an individual in your identity. There is also this complete refusal to remain confined in that identity. When you write that you are Abruzzese, Molisano, Canadian, Que-*

becois, Italian, North American, you are like someone who desperately accumulates qualifiers and yet who is fully aware that none of these adjectives can ever satisfy you. On reading that passage, I saw you spreading yourself about. And yet this man who is fiercely running after his own identity will eventually leap into the river of loss and stand there look at himself scattering away. The only homeland you seem to have is exile.

A.D.: It cannot be exile, since I am not an exile. I am here. When I go to Italy, I feel totally Italian. When I go to Paris, I feel totally Parisian. I have never felt like someone in exile.

D.B.: *Do you see yourself as someone who is always on the move?*

A.D.: I feel, like you said, fragmented. A person breaking up into pieces, fragments of himself flying everywhere, well, that person is me. This is why I love the city. I need to see people. I need to be in contact with people. I need to laugh and talk about everything and nothing at all. The time I spend with people gives me more satisfaction than all the hours I spend by myself, when I am at home or on the road. The city enables me to come into contact with men and women who will help me criticize myself. That sort of criticism is impossible in the country, because the country can offer you only a handful of neighbors. I need more than that. I need to see the neighbor breathe. I want to feel that, one day, he might, if he were upset with me, kill me. That is what living in the city means. The rules of city life are cruel and harsh, and the margins of error slim. That is what it means to be free in the city. The more we are, artistically speaking, prisoners, as Robert Bresson says, the greater is our freedom.

B.D.: *Is there a city that stands out more than others?*

A.D.: Montreal.

B.D.: *How do you, retrospectively, view your moving away from Montreal? It must have been very hard for you to leave. Your decision to leave was political, wasn't it?*

A.D.: I do not want to talk about it. I left so that I would not make enemies. Many people, dear to me, did not see things as I saw them, or was it that I no longer saw things as they did? I am not sure. I got scared. What truly weighed heavily on the balance of the decision to leave was that, as I child, I felt this burning need to leave Montreal. I can't explain it. Already, at five, I knew this city like no one. At six, I had devised a way of getting on the bus without paying. I learned to survive alone in this city. I used to tell myself that before I died I would get to know every part of Montreal. I know few people who know Montreal like I do. I left a piece of me on every Montreal street.

The Writer's Position and Point of View

D.B.: *On the back cover of* En Italiques, *we find: "Un essai? Oui d'une certaine manière. Mais l'essai d'un poète." (A book of essays? Perhaps. To a certain extent. But the essays of a poet.") Do you agree?*

A.D.: The publisher wrote that. He waited ten years before he published that book. He was really afraid to publish it.

D.B.: *Was he scared of creating a scandal?*

A.D.: Maybe. The book should have come out in 1991. And throughout the years he eliminated many essays that had been included.

D.B.: *You were doubly censured. By the publisher and by time: for time too can act like a censor.*

A.D.: It was censorship. I don't understand since every essay in that book had been commissioned and published by Quebecois magazines. Nevertheless, I am extremely grateful that he did finally publish the book.

D.B.: *Many of the essays seem outdated. The book should have come out earlier, it would have had the impact it ought to have had. Not that the ideas are not interesting to read, but the essays have lost the polemical edge they had when they were first written.*

A.D.: I do not agree that the essays are outdated. I have been living off those ideas for almost a decade, by giving conferences, lectures, and interviews. The note that these essays were written by a poet, and not a scholar, was the editor's idea of warning the reader that I should not be taken seriously. But I am very serious about those ideas.

D.B. *It was clearly a rhetorical attempt at diminishing the scope of your ideas.*

A.D.: Clearly.

D.B.: *Because there is this ever-present image of the self-portrait in your texts, I sometimes find it difficult to separate the I-narrator of your novel from the I in your essays and the I in your poems. What makes you decide what genre you will write in? Why do you decide to write an essay instead of a poem? In your case, it wouldn't make a different since your writings are a hybrid of all genres. Your novel is filled with conceptual thinking; your poems express complex ideas, your essays are lyrical, though maybe less lyrical than one would expect from you.*

A.D.: The editor removed all the lyricism in the essays. She thought that the lyricism would interfere with the seriousness of the essay form. We quarreled for five years on what tone the book was to have. The French version of the essays is quite different from its English version. The essay form is for me the most personal of all the genres, and poetry the least personal. It is a paradox but that is how it is with me. I want the poems to be personal on the level of content, but they should remain at a distance of my personal life. I will never let myself go in a poem. There is no *I* in my poetry. The *I* used is either a *you* or a *we*, it is never me.

D.B.: *You have just finished your second novel. What pushed you to write a novel?*

A.D.: Writing a novel is an experience unto itself. *Avril ou l'anti-passion (Fabrizio's Passion)* is a real novel. It is the baroque in motion. I wanted *Avril* to be something simple in a fragmented form. With this second novel, *Un vendredi du mois d'août (A Friday in August)*, I chose the *récit* form. It is surprisingly linear. I did what I said I would do in *En Italiques (In Italics)* and *L'autre rivage (The Other Shore)*. I chose to be extremely personal and gambled with my real life. It is the most intimate piece of writing I have ever done. It is truly *"mon cœur mis à nu"* (my heart laid bare), even though details in the novel are fictional. To avoid hurting people I decided to invent certain things.

D.B.: *It is true: in prose a cat is a cat. It is very cathartic and frightening in many ways.*

A.D.: For a long time, I was unable to finish this novel. Something kept escaping me, and I could not put my finger on what this thing was. At first, influenced by Marie-Claire Blais, I presented the novel as one long sentence. But I had to come to the conclusion that this sort of ornamental writing was not me. One day, talking with a young writer, a solution appeared before me. She told me that she had liked the fragmented form of *Fabrizio's Passion*. She suggested that I divide my next novel into twenty-five chapters, which is what I finally did. The form is linear, but the motor behind the work is baroque. There is no way for me to be anything but fragmented and baroque.

The Book Crisis

The present crisis in the book industry was in the making from the word *go*. It is the natural consequence of colonialism. The same way as the verb tense of the two preceding sentences confront one another, so must one culture confront a second culture, not through war or hatred, but with a strong dose of honesty and humility, for it is from this confrontation that a pacific remedy will arise.

If one looks at what draconian measures the U.S.A. had to invent in order to cut itself off from the British literary invasion – publishing British writers without paying royalties – it becomes clear that our government has no other solution but to adopt some important measures that will allow our culture to survive. I use the term *culture* in its broadest sense. No one has to react like Nazi propagandist Joseph Goebbels who is said to have pulled out his gun every time he heard the word *culture*. Less sickness is advisable.

We don't have to go very far to see what possible solutions exist. We must stop pointing our fingers at bookstores as the culprits. Writers and publishers are to blame as well.

Quebec had to adopt Law 51 to enable its publishing industry to protect itself from the French invasion. This did not mean that it put a stop to the availability of books published in France. Instead, a tax is added on to foreign books making their way into the country. The percentage is something to the effect of 23% of the retail price of the original book. So a book that sells for ten Euros in France costs the Canadian reader 12.30 Euros here; that is, about $17.50. This supplement enables Quebecois publishers to sell their books at a more "reasonable" price. Without such a tax, it would be impossible for the Quebecois publisher to survive.

Quebecois books sell for a fair price, although they are slightly higher priced than their English-language counterparts. I remember as a publisher being able to sell a book that we had published in English for $10 and in French for $20 without anyone batting an eyelid. Only in English-speaking Canada are publishers expected to absorb an immediate loss, simply because their books are in English.

The retail price of a book is usually five times its production costs. If a publisher pays $3 per copy to produce a book, he or she should normally sell that book for about $15. Unfortunately, this is not what happens.

U.S. publishers follow the five times production cost rule themselves. However when they ship the books up to English Canada their $15 mysteriously becomes our $11. It is here that trouble occurs. Such a low price on American books makes it very hard for a curious reader from Canada to want to purchase a Canadian book which sells for, say, $20. A book buyer in a rush to buy a book at the airport chooses the lower-priced item, regardless of who wrote the work.

Perhaps it is time English Canada considered following the same sort of rules as Quebec does now. English-language books coming in from abroad might have to be taxed. Such a tax would not only make it easier for Canadian publishers to sell their products at a fair price, it would also encourage co-publications between foreign and domestic publishers, a practice that has enabled the Quebecois and the French public to discover authors that they never would have under the present reign of publishing monopolies.

Another problem is the ever-growing presence of "foreign" publishers in Canada, though it is far from my intention to promote nationalism of any kind. The question I ask myself is: "What impact will this trend have on our identity?" It simply does not make any sense to read a newspaper article where we find out that So-and-So once published with this tiny but respectable small Smalltown Press but now has hit the big time with a large U.S. publisher. The problem is not that the publisher is a U.S. publisher; the problem is that this publisher is a U.S. publisher *in* Canada.

Ownership is a problem even if a publishing house is just a publishing house. Samuel Beckett always published his French-language books with the same small press which with time grew to become one of the finest presses in France. So did Marguerite Duras. A press becomes important because it publishes fine literature, not because it is powerful. It is the power of these foreign publishers that make it simply impossible for Canadian publishers to survive. The ambitious writer is no fool, he or she wants power. Nevertheless, this quest for power undermines the entire industry.

It is not my intention to imply that a writer should stick to one press alone, though I strongly encourage writers to do so, but I do feel that there is a certain kind of folly at work that makes writers believe that they will be better served by publishing with a large foreign publisher operating in Canada. On this continent, most books, no matter how large the advance received for writing them, end up on the sale racks.

The gist behind this comment is to make writers realize that they should work with publishers in this country. This does not mean that a writer should be forbidden from publishing elsewhere. His book should be published in different countries by the publishers of these countries.

A Canadian-authored book published in London or New York should be a foreign book produced for the English or American markets respectively, and not used for dumping. (Imports are necessary, but only as collectable items for specialists.)

It is the close unit that a writer and publisher form that becomes a fundamental element of cultural identity. Remove one of these parameters and identity itself fails.

There are no foreign publishers in Quebec.

All the writers in Quebec publish with Quebecois publishers.

There are a handful of writers who publish in Paris, and these authors are readily available in Canada, but at a higher price (due to the book tax imposed on the product).

A writer is free to publish where he wishes, but all

books of Quebecois writers who published abroad are considered "foreign" books, not Canadian books.

There are also situations of co-publications, in which works are published in Quebec with a Quebecois publisher who then finds a fellow publisher in France. Together they produce the same book, thereby cutting the production and shipping costs.

It is this tight connection between writers and publishers that fosters Quebec's fascinating and vibrant literary community.

The vibrancy had to be cultivated, however; it did not fall from the sky.

Last but not least, the biggest problem with English-language publishing in Canada is the English language. Of course, English is a great language, but I do agree with the late Gaston Miron, who said that Canada would have been a stronger literary country had its people spoken, for the sake of argument, Iroquois; that is, a language other than French and English.

According to this argument, it is because Canada does not have one unifying language, because the majority of the Canadian population shares a language spoken by a large portion of the people living in the U.S.A., that we find ourselves in a weakened position.

Maybe future generations will devise a way to stay Canadian without having to resort to the English or French language – who can say?

But one thing is for certain, this country of ours, at least in its English-speaking quarters, is faced with a major dilemma: if it wants to survive as an independent literary community, it will have to come up with rules and regulations that will help its book industry and ultimately strengthen its cultural identity.

Literature is an inherently political commodity, precisely because it *speaks* its mind directly, no matter how indirectly, and in order to do so it needs proper political tools to able to function fully.

Je m'accuse

Culture is what is left over when all the money's gone. When culture sees money, it runs away. Luckily, we are living at a time when money is poor. Money is a commodity, like ready-to-wear clothes. Sure, I can wear designer label suits, but they fit me like the suits I can buy at any department store. It's apocryphal: money makes you rich. Money loves only the men and women it has been dining with for generations. Let's not kid ourselves: our banks are easily broken into. We have become more or less beggars. I am no exception. When I buy a book, I act like a beggar. The passion for buying books is long dead. It's all mechanical now.

I don't recall if I bought or stole my copy of *Paradis artificiels* by Charles Baudelaire. That was in Concarneau, summer of 1973. I remember the burning sensation I felt whenever I walked by the bookstore that carried the book which had Baudelaire's picture on the cover.

I was in Brittany, and broke. The coins in my pockets hardly sufficed to get me something to eat or drink. Every day, though, as if some god were testing me, I would run one way or another into the book. My insides were on fire. One day, instead of buying a bottle of Evian water, I decided to purchase that inexpensive paperback edition of *Paradis*. What matters about this anecdote is the passion that a book had kindled in me. Not the lack of money, just the book. A simple book. I had read *Le Spleen de Paris, Les Fleurs du mal* and especially the masterpiece *Mon coeur mis à nu,* but I knew absolutely nothing of Baudelaire the essayist.

The love affair I experienced with that particular book would repeat itself only once or twice: in 1970, when I fell upon a copy of Leonard Cohen's *Flowers for Hitler,* at George's bookstore, at the corner of Sainte-Catherine and Saint-Mathieu; and in 1976, when I discovered by chance a copy of a chapbook, *Nattes,* by Philippe Haeck (whom I would translate in the 1980s), in a convenience store at the corner of Papineau and Mont-Royal. That passion has since subsided, even though I keep on spending $2,000 plus a year on books. That fire for books has been extinguished. When I purchase books, it is not passion anymore, but a sense of duty. As a writer I have to read what is out there. An anti-Pennac.

Sometimes I even dare buy a bestseller (how I detest the word) which, more often than not, turns out to be a letdown. Bestsellers usually bore the hell out of me. They are to literature what ready-to-wear clothes are to fashion; that is, things that we ought not take too seriously. What is most striking is the fact that I can pin a date to this phenomenon of "cultural cooling." This terrible shift occurred between 1984 and 1986, when "large publishers" (another terminological aberration) set out to convince me that bestsellers had become great literature. In the late 1980s, such an idea would have made most readers of books chuckle. By the year 2000, I realized that, if I publicly denounced a bestseller, I would be quickly derided for being a sour grape. James Joyce said that he had written *Ulysses* with the idea in mind that he would die once it were completed. How does one celebrate nowadays the death of this sort of writer?

Quebecois poet Lucien Francoeur wrote somewhere: *I write like I live: badly.* Patrick Straram, who I consider one of the great writers in Canada, quoted the line numerous times. What phrase would be more appropriate today: "I write like I live: a slave trader"?

Whatever attracted me to literature still attracts me. I love books that are daring, vulgar, mean, snobbish, disillusioned. Literature is the kind of person we love during the night but who, in the morning, we would not introduce to our parents or friends. Literature is the mean kid on the block who drove teachers and priests crazy. Great literature is that thing we, blushing a deep red, bring to the person behind the cash register who sneers: "You are spending your hard-earned money on *that*?" It is specifically this aspect of the forbidden fruit that is lacking in contemporary literature.

Nothing depresses me more than seeing a writer dreaming about going to bed with a literary award. Where are the Jean-Paul Sartres, the Leonard Cohens, the Roland Giguères, the Gilbert Langevins, writers who wrote for reasons other than to sleep with an award?

Sartre turned down the Nobel Prize in 1964 (Pasternak did so in 1958). Which writer today would turn down an award? Writers have become fixated by glory; they want to be paid a lot of money for what they scribble down in the privacy of their homes. There are poets who end up on a psychiatrist's bench because they did not win an award.

What has disappeared is the writer who writes for himself, for his friends, or for his girlfriends. In 1726, Jonathan Swift coined the terms "prostitute writers." Obviously, writers who act like paid lovers have been around for some time.

Authentic literature cannot be bought. There is never enough cash to purchase literature that completely dismantles our mental and moral frameworks. This sort of literature can be shared, borrowed in secrecy, stolen, but it can never be had with the exchange of money. It is too monumental, too unpalatable, too generous for us to find on every shelf of every bookstore.

I am afraid to admit it, but Quebecois literature has become, in the last decade at least, very English Canadian in this respect. I have noticed a handful of my literary acquaintances slide down in frantic descent towards the imitation of what is considered normalcy in the book industry in English-speaking America. If truth be told, this new attitude in Quebecois letters originates no doubt more in Paris than in Toronto or Ottawa.

The manner in which grants are being distributed in this country surely affects the literature that these grants subsidize. We create these mammoth spotlights that are meant to white out the local twinkling candle lights. The idea behind this strategy, for it is deliberate, is to eliminate diversity. As the market area for readers is limited, we have chosen to offer quality (usually from abroad) versus quantity (usually local). Hence, the refrain that there are too many books being published in Canada. The real question is: too many books for whom?

To write about Saint-Michel in Montreal is too local; but to speak of Fifth Avenue in New York is universal. Let us not forget the price one eventually pays for success: the Beatles and the Rolling Stones do not own the rights of many of their own songs. The book machine has imposed on readers everywhere firm criteria on what is sellable and what is not. There is a rumor that in Italy certain publishers decide on who will be the next bestselling author, not on the quality of the work, but on the stage appearance of the writer. And surely, Italian publishers are not alone in acting in this grotesque manner.

Often publishers intentionally establish a hot theme with the potential for becoming a bestseller and then seek out the craftsman to produce the fated work. These hand-picked workers are also handsomely recompensed. Like prostitutes. Why not? The entire country is happy and satisfied. "We got what we wanted. You need a book on blacks, we got one in the making. You need a book on gays, no problem." Cultural sanitation is overwhelming. All we now need is for the press to cheer: "A masterpiece." A thing easily accomplished. Add an agent and we've got an award-winning writer. Agents have a fortress at the Frankfurt Book Fair protected by the police. The day I saw that the army was needed to protect books, that is the day I knew that literature was in danger. Television and the Internet will never kill the book. What will kill the book is the book industry, which bleaches literature and makes books irrelevant. Millions of trees are felled for the creation of these dispensable confections, all skillfully crafted with little to say.

Hubert Aquin was right when he told critics that the writer was not a grammarian. What most of contemporary literature has to offer is expert workmanship, refinement, proficiency, and sophistication which ends up being boring, inconsequential, ineffectual, and forgettable. Nonetheless, the bigwigs of our dailies are hired to remind the skeptical reader how newsworthy this breathtaking achievement truly is. Read the repetitive quotes (using the same nouns and adjectives) on ads and book covers to see my point. If every book is a masterpiece, then please make sure mine is a failure.

Reviews. What to call the things we read in our weeklies? If they are not riddled with hatred, they usually end up sounding like paid advertisements. There are so few reviews about the Canadian literary production, that I have yet to find out – I who work on a daily basis in the field of books – what books are being produced in this country. I should know, but I don't. It's impossible to know. Imagine in what state of ignorance the occasional reader finds himself.

I do not wish to pass for someone who advocates regionalism. Between stubborn provincialism and money-hungry universalism there lies an unexplored territory. What is being done there? One raises his head after skimming through newspapers with the notion that this country produces few books. I read somewhere that Canada publishes around 8000 titles per year. Where are they? Where can we read about them, I mean, outside specialized magazines no one reads? *Les quotidiens, i gionarli,* newspapers: aren't they supposed to talk about the lives and works of this country's citizens? One is loath to admit that perhaps we hardly exist. Yes, I have learned my lesson: it has been reiterated aloud so often. Quality comes from abroad. Indeed, are we serfs?

Creative writing classes, I fear, frequently encourage new writers to emulate the skilled laborers of ready-made literature. Even I, who teach scriptwriting, am faced with students who demand that I reveal the tricks of how to write "off-the-rack" scripts. When I tell them about where my tastes lie, they disparagingly brush off the names of giant filmmakers, totally forgotten today, yet necessary to their education. "You're a heretic," they say, and I am ready to accept that remark. But it is all of us – the consumers of the ready-made – who carry the blame for the mediocrity we read everywhere. We scream against pornography, all the while ordering truck-loads of it, and accusingly point our fingers to its producers for being shameless.

It is we who are responsible for the existence of this sort of literary pornography that will tomorrow sell the skin of our innocent children.

"Je suis malade" ("I am sick"), sings French pop singer Serge Lama.

"I need help and bad."

It will take generations before we see a literature *engagé*, the kind that Sartre dreamed of.

My generation invented New Age indifference, and my children have rerouted my dreams of getting closer to nature by genetically modifying nature and selling it back to me for a profit.

It took me twenty years to become a vegetarian; all of a sudden, I find myself eating tomatoes made of shrimp.

Jean-Luc Godard, in one of his books, writes that "forgetting is also part of the holocaust."

Cultural amnesia, however, is not ataraxia.

We have elected our demagogues.

We have unlearned the lesson that true literature once taught us: surprise the reader with utopia. Even the monster, the kind only we can create, would have a hard time awakening us to our folly. If there is money to be made, we'll find a way to package it accordingly.

We are burning books every day, in every part of the world. We have given this an official name: pulping. Unsold books that can't be remaindered (another one of those mysterious terms from the book industry) are shredded in order to make way for our next bestseller.

What is the use of complaining to the editors of newspapers? Your letters will never get published. Why should they get published? The best way for us to get rid of a disgruntled serf is by offering him a lot of money so that he shuts up.

I have been brainwashed to keep my remonstrations to myself. The cruelest prison for any person of action is silence.

Global capitalism, a fine invention, has promised everyone freedom of speech. What you don't know is that it has silenced the people who were willing to listen. Speak as much as you want. There is no one to listen.

I am the solitary writer blabbing away in my little corner, connected to the entire world, but no one is out there to listen.

It is all my fault, I say to you.

I am to blame for what has happened to books.

I am to blame.

Je m'accuse.

Talking with Students

Students: *There have been numerous academic essays and critical reviews written on your work, teachers are using your writings in the classroom, students are reading your words, papers are presented at national and international conferences on what you have written and said, your written words are quoted . . . How do you reconcile this evidence with your view that you are not being recognized? Do you only value attention if it is manifested in the mass media?*

Antonio D'Alfonso: Artistic recognition has nothing to do with the success promoted by mass media. Of course, I have, like any writer, a desire to have my fat ego caressed but I know that ultimately this is not important. In fact, success might hamper creative activity. I am touched that people have written about my work. That certainly has given me legitimacy, first of all in my own eyes. I can still hear my parents asking: "But what are you doing?" I can now honestly reply: "I work in the world of books." When I say that we are not being recognized, I mean very simply that none of the Italian-Canadian writers are not truly recognized *as writers.* We are seen as freaks. We get accolades, but accolades do not satisfy the need for cultural response. The act of writing is communal. I write to exchange ideas with my readers, some of whom are writers as well. I write with the same purpose as when I write letters. I feel a very immediate sense of communion with the reader of my letters. I want to laugh, I want to seduce sexually, intellectually, I want to be arrogant, I want to cry and be humble. I want to be myself and offer this experience of being myself to other people. It is this sense of exchange that I feel is lacking for Italian-Canadian writers. There is no readership for our works. Many people read us for sociological reasons. We are social aberrations, and professors who read us do so in order to see if we fit into the parameters of what they think it means to be multicultural. Mostly, we get tossed aside as garbage. Let's face it: few reviewers in English-language magazines have ever written about us with any sympathy. I say this candidly because I am able to compare what is offered us by English Canada to what is offered us by French Canada. No matter what people say, English Canadian criticism is culturally intolerant. When you think that Canada is made up of primarily non-English peoples, it comes to me as a shock when I notice how incredibly mean we Canadian literati really are. The Quebecois and First Nations carry on their shoulders centuries of indifference; we are only starting to realize how large the bag on our shoulders actually is. If it were not for French Quebec, I would never have continued to write, and even less so become a publisher. It was the likes of Gaston Miron, Patrick Straram, André Roy, Nicole Brossard, Claude Beausoleil, Philippe Haeck, and Paul Bélanger who gave me the courage to continue to write. These writers were my companions and my colleagues. I have met only one person after ten years of living in Toronto who comes close to giving me the sort of support the

Quebecois writer gave me: Barry Callaghan. Barry suffers from ostracism, and he is a Torontonian. There is no sense of community in English Canada. Writers become writers as others become businesspersons. It's a job. People write from 8:00 a.m. to 12:00 p.m. and then they punch their card in the box of their desire for success. The recognition I feel is lacking is not the success many writers aspire to. What I crave is the reader as a friend. A companion. Someone I can exchange my ideas and fears with. I would probably not have written a single word if I had not known French Quebecois literature. Every chapter, every essay I have written were things I was invited to write. An essay like "Une place sur terre" ("A Place on Earth"), as disturbing as it was for me to write, and for François Hébert to ask me to write it, is meaningless in English-Canadian literature. English Canada knows Italians have no place in this country, and it would certainly never have asked me to write a piece of that nature. There isn't a magazine or newspaper that deals with such issues on this side of the country. I used to write poems after reading Montreal's daily, *Le Devoir.* I would get so upset by what I read that I would sit down and write a letter to the editor, which would *always* get published. The only time I wrote a letter to the editor here, the *Toronto Star* edited it to such a degree that it expressed the exact opposite of what I intended. Thanks to *Tandem* and *Corriere canadese* I am starting to feel what I used to feel with *Le Devoir.*

S.: *Your novel,* Fabrizio's Passion, *is being translated into Portuguese. How will the Portuguese translation capture the multilingual character of the original novel?*

A.D.: Translation has nothing to do with the original piece of writing. Translation is a cultural activity that works like a barometer of the cultural health and sanity of a country. Without translation there is no culture. I am touched that *Fabrizio's Passion* is going to be translated into Brazilian Portuguese. It is even more encouraging because I do not know the translator, Andrea Pagano. I have never met her, and I do not know the Brazilian publisher. This translation is being done simply because Ms. Pagano felt that this modest novel of mine moved her. Where she found it and how she put her hands on it remain a mystery to me. One day I received an e-mail from her, in which she asked me if she could translate my novel into Portuguese and Spanish. I wrote back saying that yes she could. Then she explained how she thought my novel had similarities to a few South American novels she was working on as a scholar. I do not know what novels she is referring to, but I do not find this resemblance farfetched.

Brazil is very much like Canada and the U.S.A.: a pluricultural society. The unfortunate difference between these countries is that half of Canada's population believes it is British. No one in Brazil thinks of himself as Portuguese. They are lusophone, they belong to the Portuguese-speaking world community. That's the main difference. Canadians do not view themselves as being part of the anglophone world community. They think they *are* British. And when minority Canadians who speak English do not think of themselves as British servants then they blindly embrace the U.S. way of life. Canadians have a serious identity problem.

Gaston Miron once told me that Canada would not be the confused country it is today had it purposely chosen to speak Iroquois. The fact that many Canadians speak and write in English is a great drawback to this country's identity. Quebec does not suffer from this identity illness. Not yet. The Quebecois choose to speak French; they don't have to. Quebec's present problems stem from other historical factors.

But to go back to the comparison between Canada and Brazil, I would like to point out how all American countries share one common denominator. They are not nations built on territorial identities, but pluricultural countries composed mostly of immigrants and the children of these immigrants.

This is the essence of America. The failure to connect all the citizens of this continent on a pluricultural basis has prevented America as a whole from attaining cultural maturity. Some individual countries more than others have reached a higher level of cultural growth. Brazil is one of them. The U.S.A. too. But it is the U.S.A. that has, because of its linguistic and military powers, hampered both American continents from achieving unity. Putting aside U.S. military policies, the U.S.A. might have managed to fashion a cultural world view that would have been more fruitful today had it been, say, German-speaking, as it almost became at one point in its history.

I am not sure that the English language is a generous language, nor that it is a more democratic language, as some claim. It is a domineering language, and Canada is, quite frankly, just a pawn in the scheme of things linguistic. Had it chosen French or if it one day chooses, for instance, Italian as its official language, maybe our pluriethnic imaginary worlds will flourish more vibrantly.

S.: *In this collection, there are essays on* In Italics, Fabrizio's Passion, The Other Shore, l'Apostrophe qui me scinde ... *Which of your works have given you the most satisfaction during the writing process?*

A.D.: I have always approached writing a poem, an essay, or a section of a novel with a similar passion. There is something in me that makes me get up in the middle of the night and sit down in front of a notebook and start writing. The four books that you mention, each took many years to compose. *L'Apostrophe* took twenty years to finish. There are parts of this collection that were with me since the early 1970s. Some were even published in magazines before they took on their present shape.

Writing is a tool that helps the human being to look at life in a different way. I have never written a single word for the sake of writing. Perhaps the fact that I am an editor and publisher has allowed me to be a little more discriminating about what sort of text I want to produce. I wish I had more fantasy in me, by which I mean *fantasia,* a lighthearted approach to creativity. I feel my writing does not always reflect, except for some texts, the person I am in my everyday life; that is, in appearance. It's true I am a jovial type of person, and readers expect to find some aspect of my joviality in my works. When they don't find it, they are somewhat disappointed. I wish I could write more comedy. But I can't. Seriousness has always been, and is still in me. This is the reason I write. I am therefore, in spite of myself, a cerebral writer. Maybe it is my way of reconciling opposites that vie within me.

Writing has enabled me to become a better person, I think precisely because it reveals the various facets of my person. I would certainly not be who I am had I not written a single word. Being able to comment on what I see and believe is the essence of all I have done as a writer, for I am a writer of social and cultural commentary. Writing has given me the chance to expiate the worst parts of my being. Poetry is the exploration of the cultural mind; the essay the intellectual mind; the novel the emotional mind. Being a publisher permits me to unveil the physical mind. To paraphrase Gurdieff, these activities are my way of attaining the higher intellectual and emotional centers of my being.

I have no patience for the bureaucratic writer, that career writer who sets himself or herself the goal of fashioning a poem or a novel in the best traditional way possible. In fact, I have a strong revulsion for this sort of writer: there is nothing more annoying in my eyes than to have to read the product of a conniving mind. One writes to change the way we behave as a species, not to better the sestina, the terza rima, or the sonnet. The same applies to the journalistic essay or the plot-driven novel. I get bored by what the writer expects from me. No, clever writing does not make me smile. I dislike the ingenuity of clever craftsmanship.

What will definitely kill the book is the economic suprastructure based on literary craftsmanship. The writer is no longer a sage, but a public scribe. He no longer is asked to foretell the reactions of the gods to human behavior. The modern scribe simply becomes an accountant who files the income tax forms of the citizens of a nation.

S.: *Guernica Editions is your career and your livelihood; writing is your passion. You've provided a medium for many writers by founding Guernica over twenty years ago. Should you have focused your energy on your own writing only? How would you do things differently, if you could?*

A.D.: I ask myself these questions every single day. In the end I must admit to myself that it is my work as a publisher that has given me the passion to remain a writer. I fear that without Guernica Editions I would have turned out to be a career writer, a bureaucrat of literature.

Of course, the price to pay is that I have written less than I could have, for if I would have written every day, which I don't do, I could have written a lot more.

Still, I think I am prolific. T.S. Eliot wrote about 2000 verses; Gaston Miron one book of poetry and prose. The same is true of Leonard Cohen and Léo Ferré.

Then, at the other end of the spectrum, we find Jean-Paul Sartre who could not stop writing. He still managed to produce, if not the ultimate literary product of this century, at least a major sample of the very best.

It's not necessary to write much. It's not even necessary to write well. What is needed is to write what you have to write. Jean Renoir, the French filmmaker, said that we all make the same one film. Once you come to accept this essential truth about self and creativity, the desire to produce a book a year becomes irrelevant, if not absurd.

I am happy if I can produce one good poem or one important essay a year. As long as what I do fulfills both a need for self-gratification and social change then I am more than happy with myself. What is fundamental to understand, and I have come to realize this only recently, is that by being an editor and a publisher I am fulfilling the need to write about certain issues, or in a certain form, by publishing the works of other writers.

The day I published the complex poetry of Pasquale Verdicchio I no longer cared to deconstruct language. Once I published the emotional poetry of Gianna Patriarca I no longer felt the need to talk about my Italian background in a certain manner. Being the publisher of many fine writers exorcised me. Every writer I have published has pushed me ahead into a new direction. When people ask me: "Why don't you write more satire?" I reply, "But I have: go read Mary Melfi." "But it's not you," and I say, "Yes, it's me." There is a fair chance that without Guernica some of these works would never have seen the light. This is why I easily lose my patience when I hear people talk of Italian-Canadian literature without once mentioning a Guernica writer. Many do. Even today. Even though Guernica has published over 200 titles by Italian Canadians.

Whenever the press or students talk about Italian-Canadian writers they usually mention one that is not published by Guernica. I take such oversights as a personal offense. It's like talking about pasta without mentioning durum wheat.

S.: *You belong to the generation of Italian-Canadian writers who did some groundbreaking things. What does the future hold for writers of your generation? For Italian-Canadian writing?*

A.D.: Nothing much. I am not an optimist like Filippo Salvatore. Without serious social rights no ethnic group in America will survive on an artistic level. Without a new generation of Italian-Canadian Guernica writers there is no future for Italian-Canadian literature. For what will eventually happen is what happened in the past. All of this effort will turn to dust and that dust will be easily blown away. And do not even think for one moment that one or two writers will survive. None will survive.

Look at the U.S.A. where Italians were able to produce some of the most important works of that country: none have survived. Think of *Christ in Concrete* by Pietro Di Donato which, when it came out, was said to be more important than *The Grapes of Wrath*. Today it is out of print. It only exists in the mind of a handful of university professors. No matter how hard they try they will never give it the life it lost. The same is true of *Son of Italy* by Pascal D'Angelo which I personally consider the best work by an Italian North American (along with *Ask the Dust* by John Fante). Guernica just reprinted *Son of Italy;* it had been out of print for many years. John Fante is published by a small press in California. Rightly so. No one else seemed to care for his brilliant writings.

The only reason there is a Quebecois literature is because Gaston Miron worked extremely hard to make sure that there would be such a literature after he died. Gaston Miron was the first secular publisher in Quebec. He founded his press L'Hexagone in 1953. The future proliferation of Quebecois works stems from that single fact: Miron and his press. Without Miron, all we would have known of Quebecois literature would have been mostly minor Catholic writers.

For a literature to exist it is necessary to have a social structure that can keep it alive and well. Without the concerted efforts of Gaston Miron who assiduously attacked the federal government on all fronts, there would be no Quebecois literature as we know it today. It's incredible to say, but this is the simple truth. He alone made sure that the usual group fighting from within would not destroy the major cultural project he set out to launch. His press produced works by authors who influenced an entire generation of writers who would, in turn, created their own presses. But everything in its time. Writers branched out only once L'Hexagone was assured of its own survival. The Quebecois intelligentsia was very much aware that destroying Hexagone would have brought about the death of Gaston Miron. And killing Miron would have brought about the demise of the left-wing movement which is responsible for Quebec as we know it. Gaston Miron did not have to do what he did: he was a major poet and that sufficed to guarantee him a place in the pantheon of poetry. But he worked his ass off to make sure that people understood what was really at stake.

The same applies to the Italian communities of America. Or to any minority group for that matter. Without a conscious effort on the part of the community, without the will for survival, there will not be a tomorrow for the community. Culture stays alive only if we want it to stay alive. I am afraid to admit that Italians don't really want Italian culture to stay alive.

In English America, Italains want to become British. In Spanish America, we want to become Spanish. In Portuguese America, we want to become Portuguese. In French America, we want to become French. The only real solution to our survival is to become Italian. Not Italian from Italy, but what I call Italic. If people find this idea of the Italic too anarchist in spirit, then they should simply try to become Italian Canadians or Italian Brazilians. But for this to happen we need civil rights. I mean real rights protecting all our liberties. This sort of talk is not very much in style nowadays. Critics accuse me of being a purist. I don't give one damn about the purity of a people. All I ask for is for the older generation to have the right to teach the younger generation ways of staying Italian in America. But there is a rebirth of the myth of the melting pot across the world. Its new name is globalization. To speak of minority rights is to go against the grain of what it means to be modern (whatever that means).

There is a lot of work still to be done, there is a lot of serious meetings still to be had before anything truly durable will come about. Without this sort of conscious and concerted effort, all we'll ever become is an ephemeral curiosity. I am not sure if it is already too late to repair the irreparable, but time is running out quite rapidly.

S.: *What do you think of the new generation of writers following in your footsteps? What do you think is their role and what will be their legacy? What advice do you have for them?*

A.D.: It's very difficult for me to answer this question without again presenting myself as a dull pessimist. English Canada does not have a real social project, at least not the way Quebec does. Without this sort of cultural awareness the new generation of Italian-Canadian men and women will grow up with one thing in mind: becoming good capitalists. What is lacking in English Canada is a radical social consciousness. What has allowed Quebec to grow into a complex society is the constant confrontation between right-wing and left-wing groups within a single community. There are only right-wing groups in our English-speaking Italian-Canadian communities. This is the legacy fascism has left us with. Emigration made sure that Italians abroad would be cut off from the left-wing movements of post-war Italy.

It has become unacceptable to speak about the left and right wing today, nevertheless these classifications have always existed in human society, in different shapes and sizes. There have always been the nomadic and the sedentary. Though it is true that culture is an outgrowth of agriculture which only people living in a set place can produce, it is also true that culture is not a stable entity. Culture has to keep on moving to stay alive. This injection of fuel can come only from the foreigner. It is the outsider's role to give new meaning to what has remained the same for centuries.

For the next generation of writers, our community must stay in touch with its nomadic past, without which it will slip into sameness. The same way L'Hexagone helped found a new way of being a Quebecois writer, by positioning itself against the then Catholic mainstream, so must people use Guernica to allow for a different way of being Canadian. People think that I am wrong to promote this particular view of the publishing industry, that it is an act of self-aggrandizement, but they are mistaken. I just happen to be the one who started Guernica. I can easily sell it to a new generation of writers. The idea is not for the new generation to have this person be their publisher. What people must understand is that Guernica exists and that it is the only viable way for the new generation to fight against the dominance of sameness when it comes to minority literature. If young writers rush to mainstream publishers to offer their goods, they will only churn out what is expected of them: stereotypes and crafty exercises of acceptable writing.

Good literature is not about sameness. It is not even about good writing, pretty syntax, and correct grammar. Good literature is about vision, and vision can only stem from the outsider's position. For this to be possible, the new generation has to accept the tautological fact that they can only be Italian-Canadian writers if they remain Italian Canadian; that is, a minority. The moment they choose to become Quebecois or British Canadians they put an end to Italian-Canadian literature.

These ideas are so simple to understand, and so difficult to accept. Every one is only too willing to embrace Canadian nationalism and to throw aside Italian ethnicity. I have always said that all nationalisms are evil, no matter if Italian or Canadian. Too many applaud me when I speak against Italian nationalism. But they do not understand what I am saying. They are always shocked to hear me say that I am an anti-Canadian nationalist as well. What counts is the minority position, and making sure that all minorities are given their full due rights.

A person who does not comprehend the complexities of the society he or she lives in can never be a good writer. Don't get me wrong: I am not professing the stance of the *writer engagé*. What I am saying is that without awareness there can be no good literature. That sort of arrogance of the ignorant can only bring about the bureaucracy of writing. And that kind of literature serves no one.

Portraits

Gaston Miron in Rome. I have just finished dinner: white Italian bread with slices of provolone, chilled Fazi Battaglia white wine. It is half past one. I am sitting in my study, with thoughts of old age. Of course, the sun is always bright, the noise of motorbikes, constant metaphors for youth. But youth, as the cliché has it, does not last forever. Talking to Gaston Miron last night I could not help thinking about how age has finally caught up with one of Quebec's (and Canada's) most important poets.

"I have no biography," Miron tells me, "but my work is autobiographical." He laughs ironically as he tells me how he was unable to reply to any of the forty questions Chicago's International Who's Who sent him this year. "I have not attended a well-known college; I have no Ph.D. in any field; I received no medals for fighting in World War II; I have no money; I know few women; I have only my daughter, Emmanuelle, and images of myself licking envelopes and stapling jiffy bags containing books I published at L'Hexagone."

This is how Gaston Miron, founder of Les éditions de L'Hexagone, speaks. He does not smoke or drink. He is a man in his late fifties, with only two poetry books, *L'Homme rapaillé* (published by Guernica in English as *Embers and Earth,* translated by D.G. Jones and Marc Plourde) and *Courtepointes* (published by Guernica in English as *Counterpanes,* translated by Dennis Egan); but these two books have brought him very far beyond the borders of Quebec and Canada. Miron has won more prizes than any one writer in Canada and Quebec. He was given the Prix David for his life-long commitment to Quebec literature and politics. France offered him a monthly salary for an entire year to allow him to promote his work across Europe. A well-known French publisher recently offered him $15,000 to dictate his autobiography, which Miron turned down because he had "no biography to talk about."

Unlike Layton, Gaston Miron is a poet with a low profile – he never boasts about the quality of his work; unlike Atwood, he does not speak of survival, but of struggle.

There is no passivity in Miron's philosophy; all literature is struggle and the necessary expression of a people. "I carry hundreds of years of illiteracy in me," he said to the public gathered at the Villa Medici to listen to his talk on Quebec literature and politics.

Gaston Miron is now concentrating all his energy on the unification of francophones across the globe. "If we do not watch out, the world will be translating every culture on this globe from American English."

Don't get me wrong: Miron is not anti-U.S.A. But there is a difference to keep in mind between American culture and American cultural politics. Gaston Miron is one of the most well-read minds in Canada and Quebec. His personal library is his house. He knows almost every writer alive, either personally or in writing.

Why talk about Gaston Miron today? There are two reasons. First, Miron, who fought for national identity, is now fighting for internationalism: "Once you discover what makes you different from others, it is your task to impose that difference on the world, literally." Second, Miron's work has been badly reviewed recently and this raises the old problem of the lack of serious English-Canadian book reviewers. (Fortunately, Quebec has a tradition of conscientious book reviewers.)

Miron is more than what has been written about his work so far. His writing has been belittled by careless thinkers. He represents the best of what literature was in the 1950s, 1960s, 1970s, and 1980s in Canada, and it is more than the right moment to thank him for what he is doing for Quebec (and Canada).

It is painful to read and listen to people disrespectful of Miron's poetry just because it is no longer in style. Criticism has, as one of its tasks, the putting of literary works in their public perspective. How does a critic speak about a work that is different from whatever he thinks a literary work should be? Everything in Canada (perhaps less in Quebec – for difference is at the base of literary tradition there) works against the expression of otherness.

Books coming out in English Canada are so different today that literary magazines – most subsidized by university money – prefer reviewing books produced in and by other countries. There is nothing wrong with reviewing foreign writers, as long as writers working in

Quebec and Canada get reviewed as well, hopefully not ten months later. There is a lack of immediacy in reviews that is unacceptable. A book cannot be reviewed three years later. It has to be reviewed as soon as it is published. Taste is not inborn, it is acquired. And book reviews should teach readers to appreciate our works.

We cannot speak of Gaston Miron as we would speak of a poet born in the 1950s. There is a difference between these two writers which must be underlined – not for reasons political, but artistic. It is a question of *respect*. There is so little respect for the works of this country's writers in the minds of book reviewers.

Note: Gaston Miron passed away in Montreal, on 14 December 1996.

06.04.1999

Giulio Einaudi of Torino. It's a rainy day. The world is crying because Giulio Einaudi passed away.

For those who do not know who Giulio Einuadi is, let me say that there are very few people like him in the world today. Born in Torino in 1912, he died on 5 April 1999, at the age of eighty-seven, in his country home near Rome.

Einaudi was a publisher of books. A man who was responsible for producing some of the finest books in this century. What am I saying? More than just a producer, Einaudi was an inventor of writers, a lighthouse for those men and women stranded in the middle of the ocean, a beacon for those visionaries born after the disgraceful World War I and who were adults during the more horrid World War II.

Einaudi discovered writers like Italo Calvino, Cesare Pavese, Eugenio Montale, Elsa Morante, Elio Vittorini, Pier Paolo Pasolini. But he also promoted works in translation by foreign writers such as Thomas Mann, Hemingway, Nietzsche, Borges, Goethe, and Defoe. The booklist is long, very long indeed. In fact, Einaudi's catalogue is 5000 titles strong.

It is fair to say that without Einaudi twentieth-century literature would not be what it is today. Italian literature today would not be what it is without the Einaudi press. And I am convinced that many authors from many parts of the world would not be who they are today were it not for Einaudi's insight on what had to be translated into Italian. By offering these translations as fine literature to the Italian reading public, he was also legitimizing literature from abroad.

A publisher is a person who, without money, allows cultural things to happen. It does not surprise me, after reading all the testimonies in *La Repubblica,* that Einaudi had gone broke more than half a dozen times. Einaudi himself was not surprised. For a culture to thrive, it needs more than money, it needs people with willpower and guts, people who possess much more than the arrogance of ego: what is needed are men and women with a desperate desire to change the world they live in.

Einaudi worked in Torino, Italy. The home of Fiat –

the car lord of Italy. Incredible but true: Fiat never helped Einaudi when he found himself in great financial difficulty. After fifty years of publishing and financial despair, Einaudi founded his press in 1933, with the help of Cesare Pavese and Leone Ginzburg – he let go of his press in 1989, selling it to a large distribution firm which hired him as president until his death.

A publisher is one who attracts the energy around him and encourages the young men and women interested in culture to come up with these printed-paper objects which open up like fans to a thousand and one images and ideas, each one pointing to a different horizon. A book is a blossoming of hope.

Even when the fascists got into power in Italy, even after the fascists arrested Einaudi, along with many of Einaudi writers who had openly attacked the Italian right-wing government, he was able to produce books that would keep alive the struggle for democracy. A publishing house that does not criticize power cannot be a publishing house: this could have been Einaudi's motto.

Books, books, and more books. Einaudi continued producing books even when the books never reached the bestseller lists. (I am not sure such a thing existed in those days.) The fact of the matter is that Einaudi often preferred a non-commercial book to one that would bring him success and, perhaps, (temporary) financial stability.

Son of the first president of the Italian republic, Einaudi was both a cultural aristocrat and a communist sympathizer. He introduced Russian writers to the west, way before other publishing houses did. But he made mistakes – he refused to publish *Doctor Zhivago* by Pasternak. Were these decisions mistakes or choices that he made consciously? He did not care if he lost an author or two, he knew that one day important authors he had skipped over would eventually make their way back to his publishing house. A person of vision is rarely perfect.

Every Wednesday evening he would sit with a group of editors and writers. He would quietly listen to men and women argue about literature and politics. Always, he insisted that no one mention a word about finance. Write books and we'll publish them, he would think out loud. He borrowed from banks and friends, from whomever could help him bring down the debt which never diminished.

What a paradox! Here is a man who dedicated his life to producing culturally valuable books without ever making a penny. What is publishing today? Semi-multinationals with money galore that cannot produce anything but culturally-void garbage. It is as though culture is meant to be the poor distant relative of rich illiterate merchants.

Books often mean absolutely nothing to the majority of people. Especially not men. More than 70% of readers of books are women. Men prefer to read specialized magazines or newspapers. But books, pocket-size jewels, open up like doors to worlds you never knew existed.

Real book publishers are unique in the world. With the exception of a handful of publishers – some of whom are dead or no longer active in the business, people like Quebec's Gaston Miron, English Canada's Jack McClelland, the U.S.A.'s James Laughlin and André Schiffrin, Gaston Gallimard, France's major publisher, and Allen Lane, publisher of Penguin in the U.K. – rare are the people who believe in the printed word in book-form.

These are persons who sacrifice their lives for the survival of culture. They redefine what a particular culture is. They are able, thanks especially to paperbacks, to prove to the world that culture is inexpensive and priceless. Giulio Einaudi. Books.

I meant to write on education, but Einaudi's death has led me astray. Are we far from education when we talk about books? Not really.

There was a important meeting in Paris a week or so ago, dedicated to the gradual disappearance of humanistic studies in Europe. The same day I read the interview with Marc Fumaroli in *La Repubblica* on 25 March 1999, I met a writer friend from Winnipeg who had come to Toronto for a conference on the future of language studies in Canada. She only had bad news to share. "Fewer and fewer people are attending language courses," she said.

A few days ago, on Easter Sunday, while my ex-wife, my daughter, and I were strolling on St. Clair Street, we bumped into another writer who teaches at Humber College. He told me that there were only three job openings for political science in all of the continent. "Fewer students are enrolling in the social sciences," he said.

More and more, children are encouraged to quit art and social studies. Our society is pushing them into the whirlpools of computers and finance. This is bad news indeed. Without culture there can never be business. What are we going to sell? Money itself? War?

I fear that with the decline of culture (art and lifestyle) we will all be dozing off in front of our computer screens – secretly wishing that some disastrous virus would come and disrupt our brains lulled by too much speculating on this or that aspect of the stock market. With the decline of culture comes the decline of the middle class. Soon we will all wake up as educated slaves serving the Big Brother of virtual finance. Then who will keep culture alive and well in this part of the world?

Nick's Pain

The project of gathering Nick Palazzo's paintings into book form has been with me for a number of years. The body of work is such that I could not possibly undertake to produce a catalogue raisonné myself. I am glad that Mary Melfi has decided to take it on. There couldn't be a better person than Mary Mefli to come up with the right editorial ingredients in order to build a necessary presentation of this fine painter who passed away at so young an age. Guernica has used Palazzo's paintings on a number of our publications: Caterina Edwards' *Homeground*, Gérald Godin's *Exterminated Angel*, Alda Merini's *A Rage of Love*, Mary Melfi's *Sex Therapy,* and Carole David's *Impala.* And we will continue to do so.

ANTONIO D'ALFONSO

Here is a man whose vision is, curiously enough, the painter's counterpart of Melfi's literary vision. Both reveal life's eeriness for all to see. No, this is not surrealism, nor the scared person's judgement of what the world is experiencing, but rather a spiritual view of our decaying world. The painter is very much part of the depicted realities, much like a wartime artist. Nothing is two-dimensional anymore. Good and evil stand face to face and are exchangeable. The front, back, and sides of people and objects become transparent to the sensitive viewer. Nick Palazzo is as harsh as Soutine, as romantic as Modigliani, as religious as Rouault.

Expression surpasses self-expression, and depiction of reality exceeds simple figuration. This is the art of synthesis where, among other themes, homosexuality in its affirmation embraces Catholicism in its denial. This is the pictorial equivalent of Dutch writer Gerard Reve's literature. But the viewer is never asked to accept even these biographical elements, for what is represented is not simply the truth of *self* but the truths of all humanity.

Nick Palazzo's portraits are not portraits per se. He is not a psychological painter; his portraits are sociological commentaries of the worlds he lived in. He might have been poor in reality, but his characters were presented as aristocrats. Nick Palazzo had no time to unroll a canvas and pull it on a frame. He needed an other-worldly daguerreotype, and this is why he used simple artistboards and acrylic as his media: rapid, dispensable, inexpensive. An *essential* artist, par excellence. Life was more important to him than painting, in spite of the fact that painting was all he cared about. This is a world of contradictions, a world of syntheses. Nothing is simple, everything is composed of complex entities. These pictures are not apocalyptic images of a dying world, but its documentary.

Strangely enough, or perhaps it is not as strange as it seems, death came when the window started to divide the painter's life from the world he loved. As soon as the artist started to distance himself from his own everyday reality, he started to disappear from the canvas. Haunting images, these self-portraits, for they represent not only the end of life but the end of art as well. Yes, the white of the canvas is the artist's nightmare, not because he has no longer anything to express, but because what he had to say has been said totally. People often say that the dying know when they will die; the same is true of the artist. Artists know when their time has come. I say this to remind us that what Nick Palazzo has left us is not the potential of an oeuvre cut short, but the collected works of what he had to show us. And we should count ourselves fortunate to have witnessed this memorable artist at work.

Snatches of Conversations

07.08.1984

A thought from Patrick Straram, without doubt one of the best writers on both sides of the country: "On ne peut vivre entièrement, pleinement, qu'avec un style, qui singularise, le contraire de la conformité – un Même qui indifférencie, anonymise et stérilise, refoulant, censurant l'être, le réduisant au seul rôle d'automate" (*Blues Clair: Quatre quatuors en trains qu'amour advienne,* avec Francine Simonin, Éditions du Noroît, 1984).

("The only way for us to live fully and completely is by creating a style that will singularize us, that will let us stand at the opposite side of conformity, the opposite side of Sameness, which renders us indifferent, anonymous, sterilized, censurers of being, repressed and reduced to acting like robots.")

One plus one equals four. Not two. What happens to the plus sign and the equal sign? To the act of adding one thing to another? Even mathematics needs to change.

Nothing in one's life ever happens without reason. After my one-year stay in Mexico, I went to work in Ponteix, Saskatchewan. It is a small town southwest of Regina, composed of a French community that moved there in the early 1900s. I had been invited to keep a group of adolescents in touch with their French culture through the help of video.

My position was unique: an Italian sent from Quebec by a federal institution, the National Film Board, to help promote the French language and culture in a German and Ukrainian area of Saskatchewan. Working for over two months with these seventeen-year-olds changed my life for the better. It was there that I became conscious of who I was, where I was going, what role I was to play in the Italian community living outside Italy, in Quebec, in Canada.

In May 1984, Italian writers living and working in Quebec and throughout Canada were invited by the Canadian Academic Centre in Rome to meet for the first time. The Conference entitled "L'esperienza degli Immigranti Italiani in Canada" (9-13 May 1984), organized by Roberto Perin and assisted by Antonella D'Agostino, was a turning-point in the private lives and careers of all these writers. "Un bicchiere di vino" would never just be a glass of wine after this experience. The writers were Mary di Michele, Caterina Edwards, Maria Melfi, Alexandre Amprimoz, Fulvio Caccia, Pier Giorgio Di Cicco, Antonino Mazza, F. G. Paci, Romano Perticarini, Filippo Salvatore, and Pasquale Verdicchio. The leading specialist was Joseph Pivato.

This was the first time Italian writers in Canada realized they belonged to a group. A very united group, despite the different styles and ideas each individual brought to the forum. It was the birth of an (inter)national friendship. There were thirteen writers to explain the complexities of being Italian outside Italy. The titles of the papers speak for themselves: The Immigrant Writer in Quebec and Canada, The Woman

Immigrant: Doubly Oppressed, The Writer as Immigrant: Stranger or part of the Italian community.

Thirteen writers paved the way for a more closely-bound relationship with Italy, a way to experience "difference" in a country where differences are only superficially tolerated, a way too to fuse oneself with a country in need of external voices to listen to, as one needs a mirror to look at oneself. Country: Quebec, Canada or Italy?

Quebec is not a simple plane with two sides. It is a triangle, a pyramid, the facets of which lead to different perspectives, touching one another at thin borders, yet converging at a common summit, its base being – only a fool can believe otherwise – French mixed with Amerindian blood.

According to Statistics Canada (26 April 1983), Quebec has a population of 6,369,065 people: 5,106,665 are French; 487,358 British; 163,735 Italian.

These figures, not to be taken as sacrosanct truth, show, nevertheless, to what extent Quebec is far from being a bipolar nation. Here is a community of men and women who, unfortunately, have been oppressed. Because of this there are three Montreals: Montréal, Quebec-France; Montreal, United Kingdom-U.S.A.; Monreale, Italia. The minorities did not have to write in French. The British minority produced only two poets to my knowledge who preferred to write in French: Émile Nelligan and William Chapman. The Jewish writers who followed used English that contained only the rare flash of French culture.

It took over twenty years before writers of another

minority group, the Italian, decided to express themselves in French as well as in their own mother tongue. I stress the words "as well as" to emphasize the fact that, for these writers, writing is the final product in a chain of conscientious actions performed by conscientious persons. To write in French today in Quebec, as Marco Micone, Fulvio Caccia, Carole David, Mario Campo, Filippo Salvatore, Francis Catalano, and others are doing, is a political gesture.

It is the artist assuming his civil role in a society made up of human beings ready to discover, understand, appreciate, analyze, praise, criticize new realities. To choose to write in English in Montreal seems to be more and more, in my opinion, an absurdity. Who reads the English writer in Montreal? Who buys his books?

Yes, a writer lives neither here nor there. He is elsewhere (which is good). Still it is the most interesting decision, one filled with political connotations, that the Italian writer in Quebec can make: to write in French. This gesture determines his difference, it is his way of removing himself from the English past and placing himself in the reality of the French presence.

And yet, paradoxically, he must keep his distance from the majority. For him to synchronize this double movement of belonging to and detaching himself from the French community he must first reconcile himself to his identity, the modern Italic identity and not the tarnished nostalgic image he was taught to create for himself in order to survive. He must re-educate himself: he might want to learn Italian, read books and magazines in Italian, take frequent trips to Italy.

There are no two solutions: he either becomes what he was up till the age of ten and begins to write in Italian for the Italian public here and in Italy, or he leaves everything behind him and joins the ranks of either the French or English groups. Such an attitude, harsh in its presentation, remains the only possible way to sanity. To encourage those who think Italian is a dead language, consider this: "As late as 1960, and probably even today, Italian continues to be the most common spoken foreign language in the U.S.A., as it had been in 1950, 1940, and 1930" (Richard Gambino, quoting Joshua A. Fishman, in *Blood of My Blood,* p. 114).

Italians in Quebec and the rest of Canada have never lost contact with their Italian culture. It might be perverted, self-censured, censured by those in power, but it is still there, in their way of talking, being, eating, loving, and in creating love around them. Italians might have attended French and English schools where they were obliged to converse in another language in order to communicate with their environment; however, as soon as they returned home, they spoke in their dialects. In the case of those who studied in English schools – 75 to 80% of the Italians in Quebec and the rest of Canada – English became a convenient tool for communication between friends belonging to different peoples of different regions of Italy, where the *pura lingua* was spoken only rarely and by a very few – a language imposed by Mussolini during World War II to continue the unification of Italy of 1861.

Mussolini banned dialects. In Quebec, in the rest of Canada, in the U.S.A., English is learned in the same way

Italian is learned in Italy by the children of the Mezzo-giorno (composed of Abruzzi, Molise, Campania, Apulia, Basilicata, Calabria, and Sicily). To have a healthy Italian people outside of Italy, it has become imperative for Italians to decide where they stand and what position to take in facing the future.

As a child I, for instance, spoke my Guglionesano (Molise) dialect at home, Italian with my Italian friends, French on the streets of Montreal, and English in the classroom. This mixture of languages has had its effect on my way of being, communicating, breathing, writing. My case is not exceptional. Even my cousins and friends who never studied beyond eleventh grade know at least three languages. When it comes to writing, this myriad of everyday experiences colors the way one writes. Don't expect an Italian writer of Quebec or other parts of Canada to write like the writer who knows only French or English or, if he writes in Italian, to write like the Italians in Italy.

The Italian writer here has to create a style of his own, and once this style is found he must learn to live with it in spite of the mean-spirited criticism he will eventually encounter along the way. (The Italian writer of Quebec uses English words positioned in a French syntax to express the Italian experience, either directly or indirectly. No wonder so few Italian writers can be found in mainstream literary anthologies.) The books published by Italian writers are too many to list in this piece. It is only necessary to underline this crucial moment in the history of Italians as a people, as a creative community in Quebec and in the rest of Canada.

Italians may need to move away from their Italian neighborhoods, but they will always remain conscious of what they are. It is plain that being Italian is a cultural and psychological, more than a geographic phenomenon. With the mass emigration (more accurately called a cunningly organized expulsion) of Italians (mostly, Southern Italians) during the twentieth century, the history of Italy and its people is far from coming to an end. It has changed direction. As Richard Gambino writes in his important book on Italian Americans, *Blood of My Blood,* Italians abroad "must foster their ethnic awareness and shun temptations and pressures to become transparent people, without substance, or to drop out altogether ... To set their destiny in motion, they need to know themselves. With self-knowledge and the imagination it stimulates ... they can realize the dreams denied their immigrant grandparents and sacrificed by their culture-conflicted parents" (p. 374–375).

28.10.1987

October cold. Frankfurt Buchmesse. Thousands of books piled up one upon the other, and people strolling along the alleys of this labyrinth of enlightenment, many from the opposite ends of the world. Strange how certain literatures can be exportable, and others not.

I ask myself: "Is poetry exportable?" Some will immediately nod *yes.*

I'm not so sure that poetry is exportable. We can speculate with translations, but what value will a translation have in a different culture? What do we know of

Canadian poetry abroad? Novels, essays, stories – prose more than poetry is exportable, because it mysteriously contains something which is immediately grasped by every reader no matter which country he sleeps in.

The *imaginaire* in works of prose – that construct made up of the conscious and unconscious of a people – can be directly transmitted from one language to another, from one person to another. Certain poetry functions on a more regional level somehow, as if the universality of its experience cannot reach beyond its geography.

The novel versus poetry. What do you know of Quebec? It is more likely that the names of Roch Carrier or Gabrielle Roy will ring a bell than the names of Fernand Ouellette or Émile Nelligan. There is something paradoxical about this that pertains more to poetry than to prose. Is it a matter of money? A problem with economics? Poetry sells less than prose. Why?

The World in Translation. The leaves of books blown in the wind, the air of words cold, airports empty in their technology. Frankfurt, Paris, Toronto. A young girl reads a novel by a foreign writer translated by someone from her own culture. Culture is always a matter of translation. In fact, one can measure the greatness of a country by the books it translates. Unfortunately, we're not much of contenders in such matters. The Canadian bookstand at Frankfurt, or the Quebec stand in Paris, contains only a handful of translated books, mostly original works by original writers.

We are a prolific country. Yet we seem sad amid these great nations of translations. The larger the quantity of books translated the larger the publisher. Which publisher in Canada, in Quebec, can boast possessing 50% of the world's greatest writers translated by national writers?

There isn't one. We find the occasional title by Calvino or Rilke stranded on the bookshelves at the Double Hook or other specialized bookstore, like a strand of hair on the forehead. We are a narcissistic bunch of lonesome heroes lifting our books like flags against the wind, our eyes closed to what is happening abroad or, if open and aware of what is happening abroad, not attempting to make it ours through translation, except as epigrams at the beginning of books.

Why translate what has already been translated? Our cultural institutions insist: national books translated by national writers only, the rest is ineligible for grant money because it is not Made in Canada. We don't blink an eyelid when we say that this or that film is Canadian because it is financed by Canadian money, despite the fact that the director, the scriptwriter, or the actors (except for the symbolic hero standing in the background of the real action), may not be one bit Canadian. Nationalism is a question of point of view. A putting into focus at a particular moment for a very precise reason.

The other day a headline mentioned that in Paris 60% of the books publishers send to bookstores are returned unopened after one month. No one reads, no one goes to the movies. Our favorite film or book is our paycheck. It is our only dream, our secret unwritten poem. What began as an intended survey on the Frankfurt Book Fair and Paris International Poetry Festival ends abruptly. A book is an object we sell, a poem is something we hear once and forget or imitate in our own poem.

This only goes to show you how lonely this job of book publisher can get with time. Decades of work and nothing left in my heart except the silence of this plane taking me back to Montreal.

I am thinking of Louis Dudek, Irving Layton, Leonard Cohen, and their words are nature in my ears. On my lap sits François Truffaut's collection of essays, *Le plaisir des yeux*.

The days of anger are long gone. Even radicalism looks bureaucratic; that is to say, there are few translations and less desire to communicate.

We sit behind our lifting tables, drowsy from lack of vitamins, our skin darkened from tanning ourselves in the sun turned enemy. I'd rather not think of pollution; let me read about Antoine Doinel and how he stole his first kiss.

25.04.2002

The little that comes from literary energy. No use in moping, nor crying. I will not even try to fight my way back to the place they made me believe was mine. Nothing left except the burn of fatigue and disillusionment. You think the work is over and in fact all you've done is create a big mess. There is no list sufficiently generous, nor grant large enough to cover the debts. The bank account is emptier than you imagined.

The few I believed in – truly believed in – are gone, and the body collapses like a sore heart when listening to a magnificent song by Jacques Brel or Georges Brassens. Not sex, not even love. Friendship dies when friends die, and tonight I lift my soul to you Patrick Straram, to you Gwendolyn MacEwen, the voices die in the glass of affection offered to us by the few friends left when the party is over and the record plays on just for you.

Whimsical yes, silly yes, but sad too for literature takes all and leaves you with nothing. Books pretend to defy time. Foolish yes, sad yes, and their mathematics of tenderness leave you alone with rumors posing as poetry and sincerity.

I read this review-blurb on a book by Quebecois writer André Roy, translated by Daniel Sloate, published in English: "The only value this book possesses is as a further indication that the Canada Council grants in aid of publication should be more closely monitored, not because homosexual eroticism should be denied expression, but because bad writing should not be supported by public money." This was written by a famous English-Canadian writer (nameless) about a famous Quebecois writer who won the Governor General's Award (plus numerous other awards for poetry in the French world here and abroad.)

This sort of opinionatedness is simply unacceptable as criticism or even as a testimony of thought; it only encourages readers in this country to sink deeper into the ignorance and cultural intolerance that already fill the minds of so many.

A country and its literature is mature when it includes more than it excludes. So little is included, in my eyes, by the literary establishment of this country.

Just one look at the "recommended reading" behind the window and you will notice how narrow it is. I wonder what is meant by: "Better destroy a country than change it."

Piango, si piango quando ti vedo così distrutto, amico mio. (I cry when I see you hurting like that, dearest friend.)

Inclusion, not exclusion.

24.04.2002

Enough of hate criticism. There is no point in a reviewer attacking every book he or she does not like. A book is like a date. I sit in front of my date at a table. I either enjoy her for who she is. Or I don't.

I am not going to start asking her to get a face lift, breast enlargement, or tummy tuck. I take the person for who she is. If I am unhappy with her, I pay the bill, shake her hand, and say *Ciao*. If there is a problem here it is neither *my* problem nor my *date's* problem.

The real problem lies with dating. If I can't deal with dating, better not to date. If a reader can't deal with a book, then he/she can leave it. We must not be the type of lover who asks the woman or man in our arms to have different hands.

We must take our lovers for who they are. Listen quietly to what our date says with the same interest he or she listens to us. This is the respect you must offer the person who took the time to come out with you. To act with disrespect is hateful.

We have to bridge cultures, promote all literature. We want people to read books other than the works of our favorite authors.

12.10.1986

Trois-Rivières. La Fondation Les Forges invited forty poets to participate in its yearly Festival national de la poésie. Thirty events, beginning with an exhibition of poetry books and ending with a very well-organized Nuit de la poésie. The organizer, Gaston Bellemare, director of the Editions des Forges, and a few other people from Trois-Rivières were responsible for this week dedicated to French language poetry of Quebec.

Saturday, October. Poets gather to talk about how poetry is presently covered by the press, literary magazines, and radio stations. Each speaks about methodology and the rules of the institution that hired him. The reviewers are honest, do not hide their preferences. "Poetry has never been as well talked about in Quebec in all the province's history as it is today," says Jean Royer, former literary critic for the daily, *Le Devoir*.

Critics have their preferences, and poets are there to remind them of the fact. However, no war is ever declared. The debate becomes so calm as to bring the talk to a sudden halt. Compared to France we are fortunate. Compared to many countries we are fortunate. What counts today is the quality of the work. Let time do the rest. It will.

Later.

The hall fills with young and not so young people who have come to listen to poets read their works. Forty poets will read for no more than three minutes. But, contrary to appearances, this is not a marathon. It looks more like *The Ed Sullivan Show,* and the poets are stars against the "blackdrop" of reality. This is where you want to be tonight, for here fiction and reality marry. Here are a few of those who participate: Alphonse Piché, Gérald Godin, Paul Chamberland, Fulvio Caccia, Yolande Villemaire, Gilbert Langevin (who reads a poem by Juan Garcia), Marie Belisle, Célyne Fortin, Lucien Francoeur, Louky Bersianik, Jean-Marc Desgent, Denise Desautels, Jean-Paul Daoust, Patrick Coppens, Claudine Bertrand, André Roy, Hélène Dorion, François Charron, Bernard Pozier, Yves Boisvert, and Normand de Bellefeuille. These are just a few of the readers, just a few of the visions which spread against the darkness of the stage, lit only in four places; spotlights over four microphones positioned at the front of the stage. A memorable fête, where the individual and the collective come to unison.

No, poetry is not dead. It is alive. Though we have changed everything about it. Call it novel, short story, verse, text, prayer, or song. It has changed its face; that is, it has become what it always was: not a prison, but a manmade object, bright against the dark sky.

Who will speak about it now? Critics around the world, throw your bestsellers away and talk about those who write about your people. What is this sickness that makes you believe that the grass is greener on the other shore? Which critic will speak about what we saw? Who will describe best what his people are experiencing? Who will write with the same fervor as when he screams "genius" about someone living abroad? Silence. The silence of criticism. The silence of lack of self-love.

01.07.1997

Nothing good can ever come of hatred. And the hatred of self, community, and peoples that we have been offered under a rubric "Insight" does not even deserve these few lines. Italians who have lived on Grace Street for fifty years have asked me to write this note. They are terribly upset to see Italians depicted so shamefully by a "Canadian." They sense Italophobia. They are not totally wrong. They know how to decipher hatred in any language.

If one thinks about it, who can blame them for being so outraged? That this article should be published by the city's most important newspaper during a festive time seems quite suspicious. It is a slap in the face. What is this newspaper telling its readers?

Giovanni Caboto's arrival to Newfoundland had just been celebrated; for the occasion, the Italian President came to visit Canada, as did the Queen of England. It is Canada Day! This should be a moment of rejoicing and unity.

The writer, daughter of Italian immigrants, writes that she is astonished to hear people speaking another language on St. Clair Street. When she felt her shiver of Canadian patriotism in Montreal during the referendum did she not hear another language? Speaking the language of one's parents or of one's lover or of an acquaintance is not a crime, it is a sign of sharing.

The article ends with a lament on her parents' inability to read *her* text! Maybe she should take the time (to find someone) to translate it into Italian. How would her father and mother react to what she says about them? They would be as hurt as my in-laws, no doubt!

I learned Italian so that my parents would be able to understand me. It is my way of saying Thank you for the love and the great upbringing.

A word to the newspaper: Next time you need a text on Italians, please contact a writer who has some love to share. There is a community of very fine Italian-Canadian writers from St. John's to Vancouver who are only to willing to share their knowledge and love with other Canadians.

12.07.2000

The Baroque? I call it the New Baroque. There is a great book on it by Mario Perniola called *Engima,* it is all about the New Baroque. I wrote him to thank him for having explained things in an essay form that I could only hint at in poetic terms. I will write about it one day.

My point of view differs from Perniola's somehow. The New Baroque is the application of what I call *essentialism,* a way of combining heterogenous elements whereby the vanishing point is not the spectator, not the artist but someone else living on a different plane. It can be religious, but it can also be secular. What counts is to unite on various planes different realities that normally can't be unified on a single plane.

This way the object created can only be appreciated fully when seen from a distance. This is my way of moving away from the dualism inherent in this country's civil and cultural policies. Not two, but many. Not one against the other, but the entire group vying with pleasure one on top of the other.

There is no beginning, no end. There is no north or south: everything is moving simultaneously. Not an addition like 1+1=2, but more like 1+1=4 (where + = are both essential elements of the equation).

20.05.1998

Not only the notion of Canadianness has been biased, so has the idea of young women writers.

A writer like Fiorella DeLuca Calce has written two novels, *Toni* and *Vinnie and Me.* Both published by Guernica. *Toni* was published in the U.K. as *It's A Bloody Girl* (which sold thousands copies). Both these novels have been translated into French and both were published and well received in the French milieu. Yet Fiorella's work has received no reviews in English Canada.

Precisely because the establishment press does not consider Fiorella a *bona fide* writer. The same applies to Carole David, Gianna Patriarca, Concetta Principe,

Karen Shenfield, Ruth Panofsky, Elana Wolff, Julie Roorda, Merle Nudelman, Malca Litovitz, Angela Baldassarre, Isabella Colalillo-Kates, Miriam Packer, Darlene Madott, Maria Ardizzi, Marisa De Franceschi, Caterina Edwards, Robin Blackburn, Christl Verduyn, Mary Tilberg, Jane Dick. That a woman is a poet, a writer who writes in French and is then translated, or is a poetic prose writer leaves much of the press people baffled.

This is the main problem with new Canadian voices. How to place these writers (are they real writers?) who are Canadian in spirit and citizenship but don't easily fit the strictures of English-Canadian literature?

Recently a reviewer attacked the editors of *Oxford's Companion to Canadian Literature* because they included Guernica in a separate entry. Why shouldn't Oxford have done so?

With over 300 titles and 500 authors in its catalogue, this press still does not fit the idea that the establishment has of literature and Canadianness: "The writers you publish are 'weird.'" At the periphery, therefore avoidable.

Though we have published over forty titles in French the Quebec entry does not mention Guernica at all; though we have over 300 titles, Guernica writers are reduced to parentheses.

Many writers have a rough time making reviewers understand just what it is that makes them writers. The problem lies with the idea that the press in English Canada has of what is Canadian literature. Profoundly conservative in spirit, the press finds itself at odds with the quality that is offered by writers that don't aspire to "selling out." The style, the voice, the themes appear problematic.

Mary Melfi is considered by many as one of the finest writers in Canada, yet she is rarely reviewed in this country; she has never been properly analyzed, in spite of the fact she is one of the few writers to have published three books in one year (two in English at Guernica and one in French).

I truly believe that if any project on young Canadian women writers has to be produced it must include this voice of difference. If it doesn't, then one is entitled to question the value of the project and editor. Many of these writers will outlast the more prominent writers featured in the press today.

16.11.1998

I am quite surprised by some of the comments expressed by second-generation Italians. Being second-generation myself, I refuse to reduce topics of such importance (ethnicity) to emotional babble. The moment one says that he or she is an Italian Canadian, a matter of serious consideration has been broached.

Many of these comments remind me of what critics against multiculturalism write on Canada Day: "Better to be a Brit than a sausage-eating, underarm-haired Wop." One does not become a good citizen by spitting on the citizenry of another person.

What is a truism with Italians in English Canada is how they are quick to compress the country called

Canada to only one group of citizens. Does our definition of being Canadian also include the French, First
Nations, other ethnic groups? I suspect not. Rooting
for a particular soccer team means absolutely nothing in
the scheme of one's identity. Should one reduce citizenship by equating it to eating shepherd's pie? Where
does the vegetarian fit in?

There are a number of books written by first- and
second-generation Italians in Canada that delve quite
intensively into such issues. Many still do not realize
that to become a citizen is not about switching one's
identity for another, nor is it about swapping one's ideology for another. Is this what the debate on ethnicity
is all about? I do not think so.

I presume that second-generation Italians who say
they are Canadian would never shed their Italian identity for the Amerindian one. What is basically being
expressed in many anti-ethnic commentaries is outright intolerance to otherness. It is this sort of sly big-
otry that must be kept in check. To say one is Canadian
in Ontario often implies that one prefers to be a Brit
rather than a Wop.

That one finds Italy nice or not, or that one claims
Canada to be one's home or not, is of no interest to
anyone but the person who speaks. What is important
is what sort of thoughts are moving behind all nationalistic prejudice. Funny how emotions innocently
become the source of prejudice.

Citizenry and issues of identity raise questions that
one does not answer through emotion. As Fulvio Caccia has so beautifully put it in *Republic Denied*: Italy is a

republic, Canada is not; Canadians are still very much part of a constitutional monarchy. We have here two opposite ideologies that no soccer game will make us forget.

Can people imagine that Italians, especially second-generation Italians, might have a main role in deciding what will become of the forbidden dream of a republican pluricultural Canada? Or for that matter, what role will Italian Canadians play in compelling Italy to become a decentralized country which will once and for all allow Italians abroad to assert their Italian identity without having first to pledge their allegiance to the Italian peninsula?

06.02.2000

Is the Italian language, or not, the *sine qua non* of Italian culture? There are proponents and detractors. Italians will never come to an agreement on this delicate matter. Too much seems to be at stake.

In the 19 January 2000 issue of *Corriere canadese* there was a small (and incredible) write-up about the United Nations which actually announced to the world that the Italian people could very well become extinct. Are Italians really dying out? If so, what are we Italians to do about such a frightening prospect?

I don't think that talk about language will solve anything. Language will divide Italians even more, for division is the essence of language. We should sincerely ask ourselves if we wish to hang on to language and make language the lifeboat for an entire people. Or should we look elsewhere for a solution to the problem of extinction?

Let us be clear: to say that language is *not* the main pillar of Italian culture should not be viewed as an act of vandalism. Instead, it might be another way for second-, third-, and fourth-generation Italians to participate in the survival debate. What is needed is to find a common denominator that will include as many Italians as possible. The more we are the easier it will be to find a solution to our problems. The fact that many Italians have given up the Italian language does not mean that they have chosen to assimilate totally into North American culture. Assimilation is one thing; to say that we will not use the Italian language as the common denominator for discussions on the Italian culture is quite another.

To put a restriction such as language on participation and membership will no doubt prevent an important segment of our population (the young) from joining in a debate that touches us all. To eliminate the young would be a fatal mistake. (Of course, I am upset that I can't send my daughter to an Italian day school in Toronto.)

To be a population of close to one million Italians and to have to make such fundamental cultural decisions on a daily basis means that there is something terribly wrong with our community. But I can't blame my parents for that. I may pretend I am master of my domain, but the truth of the matter is that I am no better off than the serfs of my past: we are working on land that does not belong to us.

25.11.1998

I feel somewhat ill at ease about receiving the right to vote which Italy has extended to Italians living outside of Italy. Many years ago I remember being upset about not having this right, as an Italian citizen, but today I see this right in a different light. Voting is a right that should not be taken lightly. What right have we, Italians living outside Italy, to decide what the present and future will be for Italians living in Italy? Not much. What would we say if 60 million Canadians living outside our borders were suddenly given the right to vote on what happens within our borders? One can only speculate the sort of outcome this retrograde reasoning would provide.

What quality of vote can one expect from people who have lost touch with the everyday reality of a country they once lived in?

To live in a country means to participate in creating chances that make a country, if not evolve, at least change, mature. People who leave lose touch with the issues that press upon those who stay behind. Only the men and women who live Italy on a daily basis must be given the sacred right of voting for their destiny.

The underlying trouble with the voting debate is that Italy is stuck finding old-fashioned solutions for embracing Italians living away from its territory. Should one suspect a more evil reason behind this need?

Why not give everyone *in* Italy the right to vote? Why go elsewhere for votes?

Perhaps voting is one way of including Italians *fuori d'Italia* in the democratic process. Yet what does one do with the new Italians in Italy who do not have the right to vote?

Are there secret categories of being Italian?

Voting is an outdated way of enhancing Italian culture. So is the teaching of the Italian language through its cultural institutes, no matter how marvelous these courses are. I learned more at the Italian Cultural Institute in Montreal than I ever did at university, where Italian is usually taught by uncommunicative Italians (not a bad thing per se, but somehow I can't help but conclude that maybe here lies one of the reasons why, after spending so many years trying to master Italian at university, I never truly succeeded in learning the language: language is more than the mathematics of syntax.)

Neither the right to vote nor the learning of the Italian language will solve the main problem that is tearing Italians apart. The disaster is that Italian culture is disappearing due to the lack of people who practice it.

What is the remedy? This is the question that Italians in Italy and abroad must now ask themselves.

Italy, as many other European nations, must go through a process of decentralization. That is, the centripetal forces that make Italy the center of Italian culture must be derailed. Italian culture can survive only if it becomes centrifugal, a reciprocal culture that extends beyond its borders, adding and subtracting elements of itself, in order to prepare for the new millennium. When Italy accepts the fact that Italian culture can also fully and independently exist outside its territory, Italian culture will then start to grow in a new democratic fashion.

01.08.96

> Être riche, encore une fois, ce n'est pas avoir de l'argent – c'est en dépenser. L'argent n'a de valeur que quand il sort de votre poche. Il n'en a pas quand il y rentre.
>
> Sasha Guitry,
> *Mémoires d'un tricheur*

I just read some reviews ("Rich and Ignorant") on CanStats figures. Why should we be surprised by these figures? They tell us exactly what we know already: we have truckloads of gold but nothing intelligent to say.

The problem is what is not revealed by these figures: it is this that worries me. For example, the definition of what is an Italian Canadian is totally out of date. Place of birth has very little to do with pluriculturalism. As if Italians could be defined for coming from Italy alone. A recent U.S. census has forced a change in the way people define themselves. No one has analyzed why, in 1994, only 500 Italians came to Canada. Is the fear of changing Canada's demographics to blame? We know, for instance, that a 1923 law prevented Italians from going to the U.S.A., and in so doing, almost eliminated the Italian presence in that country.

So we're rich. Big deal. We own large empty homes with large white walls with no paintings or books or CDs in them. We have long tables in our basements piled with lots of chemical-ridden foods. We pay taxes and ask nothing from the government in return: do we know that, according to universal law, for a culture to survive every citizen should be offering 1.7% of his or her tax money to culture? Do we care if and where that money goes?

The fact that Italians have money does not mean that they are any better off than other recent immigrants. Rather, I tend to believe that new immigrants, in many cases, have acquired through intelligent co-operation more rights than the Italian community has. Let's avoid making the mistake of our American cousins: wealth will buy a car but it buys no rights. If we want real rights, we will have to fight for them.

Recently, the Italian community at large (over 30 million Italians in the U.S.A., according to the revised census) had to bring a university in the State of New York to court for anti-Italian conduct (which had been going on for decades) and won. I fear that one day we will wake up to a similar situation here in our "rich" but truly "ignorant" homes.

In this pluricultural reality of ours, if the Italian community does not analyze its "shortcomings," it will find itself with a lot of money and nothing of cultural worth to buy. (In the same way one may have the right to vote, and yet have only one party to vote for.)

"Buying" is a privilege, and having privileges means that there are "rights" attached to these privileges. By "rights" I mean everything under the sky that will enable our community to mature intelligently in our aspirations *as a community.* As is obvious with all statistics,

the mirror on the social wall does not reflect individualistic well-being but the community's poor health. And
it is this reflection that makes me very nervous. For it is
the only one that counts in the long run.

We should be very careful about having money,
especially when money does nothing for the community at large.

Every time I hear that Italian Canadians are rich a
strange image comes to mind: the Poverty of Money.

We are quick to say that we are Canadians: how
many Italian Canadians have Canadian books, CDs,
videos in their homes? How many libraries, music-
stores, and bookstores can our community boast of?
Not many.

As if money alone buys class mobility, as if money
alone buys culture, as if money alone buys education!
Money itself does nothing if there is no intelligence
that clips those bills together.

If being rich means having stacks of money under
an "ignorant" bed in a large clinically-white room, then
allow me to be outrageous and say I prefer being a
decrepit, poor, educated "aristocrat."

What I've learnt from StatsCan is how complacent
we Italians in Canada truly are. Let's never forget: the
only future our children will know is what we Italian
Canadians bequeath to them in books, music, and art.
And that comes from education and schooling and
community cultural life.

An Italic in Paris

You have to separate imagination from the body. You have to, I believe, reach beyond whatever biological similarities that people arriving from one piece of land share, because politics have blurred the already blurry image these people have of themselves. I have no idea what an Italian is supposed to be. I have no idea what Italian culture is supposed to be. I have no idea what Italian literature is supposed to be.

I do not believe that Italian culture is what is produced exclusively in Italy. We find Italian culture in varying degrees in various places across the world, in countries wherein the Italian, whether or not born in Italy, has chosen to live. Perhaps the "purity" police of culture does not appreciate bastardized manifestations of culture, labeling it kitsch, but what this police corps thinks is of no importance in my eyes. I know that there are officially more than fifty million people outside of the Italian state who consider themselves Italian. And these people are entitled to an aterritorialized identity. I conclude therefore that there exist Italians outside Italy, whether the Italians in Italy like it or not. If I am wrong, then I will let others, more knowledgeable in ethnographical, anthropological, and sociological matters, come up with solutions for the survival of these millions of people. If, however, one accepts, like I do, that there are Italians outside Italy, then we should ask ourselves immediately, whether or not this population, with or without ties to Italy, has produced a significant body of literary works. I believe they have, and so I say that there exists an Italian literature that is created both in and outside Italy. Who are these Italians?

The term *Italian* seems pretty inadequate to capture the complexities of this bizarre and incomprehensible identity. I will be accommodating and bequeath the term only to Italians living and working in Italy on a daily basis. That leaves the rest of the people living outside Italy to deal with inept descriptions such as *Italianità* and *Italianness* to refer to Italians living outside Italy.

I have, from the start, rebelled against this kind of obsolete and functionless terminology and I have come to believe that, unless more study is dedicated to Italians in the diaspora, Italians will have to concede, not only failure abroad, but the demise of the Italian culture. Without a name, a thing has the bad habit of ceasing to exist. The term *Italics* that I have been utilizing for decades does not describe only the Italians living outside Italy; this term, from the beginning, was meant to encompass all things Italian, anywhere and everywhere, Italy included.

The Italic identity entails the upward movement towards an all-embracing cultural identity, one free of all territorial attachment. The Italic is to the Italian culture what, for example, the *francophonie* is to French culture.

No problem with the term *Italic* results on the general plane, since what is general is intrinsically universal and vague. It is, paradoxically, on the particular plane, limited and specific, that confusion inevitably arises. I have no idea why the particular always seems to derail, but it does. And we are going through a period of major derailment at the level of particular cultural phenomena. We have entered a time when genuine dangers have materialized both within and outside cultural centers. The enemy can be the Other, but more often than not, it is your friend, your brother. If the activities subsisting at the particular plane are to prevail, then we will need the active participation of what dwells on the general plane. For if Italianness (to use that unsuitable term) is to endure, it will fittingly need input from the global Italic configuration.

When I speak of Italianness, I include Italianness both within and outside Italy. Italian culture in Italy is condemned as well. I possess no clear methodology on how to define the parameters of this Italic configuration, but they must be something that are not grounded solely by an identity derived from territorial rights.

What I notice happening with politicians and many intellectuals is unhealthy. Their obstinacy only quickens the descent to total ethnic insignificance. Many publicize to seeing the summit of the place where we are heading; yet I am afraid to say that the carriage they are riding on is shoddy and faulty. It will never get them to the peak of the mountain. The time is right to invite the mechanics and welders of culture to quickly mend the machines of culture.

The people to blame are not the priests or the aristocrats, nor the peasants or the organized criminals, though all carry part of the blame; we have, each one of us, helped to create the ugly creature we have all become one way or another. The dangers inherent to cultural isolation only lead to the making of a more horrid creature, which will do more than just frighten the children away. Evaporation of a culture is but one face of this two-headed beast; the other is cannibalism.

Of course, these are symbols. I am trying to convey a sense of urgency, for many think that the success of some is success for all. The successful usually silence those who do not want to follow in their footsteps. To excess, what happens is that killing becomes a guessing game; it is not so much who those in power will eat, but who will be eaten once the "undesirable ones" have been consumed. Again, these are strong metaphors to express the obvious: the Other is often oneself, one's worst enemy is oneself.

The tycoons who opt for murder are usually ready for cultural cannibalism. We laugh and say that all of this is an exaggeration, that we are not like this at all. Yes, I am exaggerating; this is every bit an exaggeration; exaggeration is the hammer that strikes the nail where the nail needs to be struck. We can count ourselves lucky if we have not yet created a mirror large enough to throw back the images of what we are doing to ourselves around the world. We have not yet committed the irreparable.

Some escape; others walk in. The door of failure is the only remedy to survival. How else to describe, except through the use of imagery, the invisible thread that indisputably links so many different people living in so many different countries? This imaginary thread should be strong enough to draw together people of various cultural backgrounds in one single territory; it should also be long enough to bridge people of common background living in disconnected territories. This thread should remain invisible yet it must be tangible; it has to be real yet imaginary.

I am too much a prisoner of my own blinkers. I am only barely capable of distinguishing what in me is real and what is acquired. Neither the real stuff nor the other rubble is enough to take me towards the goals I have set for myself. To bridge both sides of myself seems a futile exercise, for what I would achieve would be nothing more than a thesis, an antithesis, and a synthesis – nothing more than the creation of a third term. But what I am striving for cannot be found in a third term. More and more I am convinced that what I am looking for lies in a fourth term, beyond the triad that is already in me.

The persons who will supply the answer are not the Italians from Toronto or Buenos Aires, nor from Rome or Sydney. The solution, and I firmly believe there is one, will come from the gathering of all these people. The Italic is the missing piece to this puzzle that we have created for ourselves. The Italic is from everywhere and nowhere. The Italic is someone whose culture need not to be invented, for he knows that true culture will ultimately prevent him from saying: "I have succeeded, I can rest." If he feels he has succeeded, this means he would have died.

That Hidden Resource Beneath the Ashes

Interview with Antonio Maglio

Antonio Maglio: *Does an Italian-Canadian culture exist?*

Antonio D'Alfonso: Yes and no. Yes, it exists. No, it doesn't because it is hidden. Let's say it might find a space for itself, under certain conditions.

A.M. *Which conditions?*

A.D.: First, it has to abandon the stereotypes of nostalgia, Mafia, spaghetti. These are hindrances which cannot be used to identify the Italian, let alone Italian-Canadian culture. Second, Italy has to accept the existence of an Italic culture, and therefore of an Italian literature out of Italy.

A.M.: *What does that mean?*

A.D.: It means that Italy should become aware that our diaspora created, out of Italy, a sort of cultural commonwealth that expresses itself in English, French, Spanish, Portuguese; in short, in the languages of the countries to where over fifty million Italians emigrated. If one accepts the existence of a Calabrian, Friulian, Sicilian, Campanian literature, and so on, one has to accept Italian-Canadian, Italian-Argentinean, Italian-Brazilian literature as well. Who said that Italian literary production abroad must use the mother tongue?

A.M.: *Awareness of the existence of Italian cultures and literatures outside of Italy also depends on how these cultures and literatures have imposed themselves in the countries of the diaspora. Has this imposition happen in Canada?*

A.D.: With difficulty. The fact that Guernica, after so many years, still lives on the editorial market is a proof in itself. But in order for me to answer your question we have to consider the Canadian reality. Canada's dominant culture, the mainstream, is Anglo-Saxon, with the exception of francophone Quebec. Let's consider the Quebecois: notwithstanding the fact that their francophone identity was recognized from the start, nobody gave them anything for free. They gained their own identity by themselves, losing battles but winning a two hundred-year war.

A.M.: *Don't tell me they won by repeatedly proposing referendums for separating from Canada.*

A.D.: The referendums were initiatives. They gained their identity by asserting their right to be Canadians who speak French, not Frenchmen living in Canada. This is an important distinction which cannot be found in other ethnic groups, not even among Anglo-Saxons. Less among Italians. Do you know what Gaston Miron, the publisher I consider my spiritual father, always said? "We North American francophones could conceivably declare war on France some day." He used "North America," not "Canada."

A.M.: *What about Italians?*

A.D.: Many of us still feel like guests in this country, not full-fledged citizens. This generates nostalgia; that is, the feeling of loss, or other commonplaces, such as the Mafia or spaghetti, just to mention the most trivial.

But those who speak and write in nostalgic terms are looking to the past. Real culture, on the other hand,

lives every day. Can you tell me what nostalgia is supposed to mean for second- or third-generation Italians?
These kids were born here, and they are free of the
stereotypes that conditioned their parents and grandparents. Their cultural identity is not limited to time: to
the war, to youth, to past regimes. They don't have these
reference points which, whether acceptable or not, are
anyway obsolete. And then we have to take stock of
something else. Culture can produce lobbies, but lobbies do not always produce culture. Having Italian
schools, Italian churches, Italian clubs, is all very well,
but this is also a way for many towards isolation,
because through these institutions one remains an Italian, never becoming an International Italian (an Italic).
These are different things.

A.M. *How can we clearly define an Italian-Canadian
identity?*

A.D.: Through the joint effort of intellectuals, opinion leaders, the media, universities. The purpose is to let
the present live, not to perpetuate the past.

A.M.: *And what is the easiest way to accomplish this?*

A.D.: By going beyond nationalism.

A.M.: *I don't follow you.*

A.D.: When one talks about Italian culture, everybody thinks of something homogeneous: that Italy is
Dante, the Renaissance, Leopardi. Italy, conceived as a
monolith, is therefore a nation, nationalistic. But our
culture is also something else.

Do you remember the famous controversy between
Pasolini and Calvino? Pasolini said that in order to
reach universalism one had to start at the regional level;

that is, to identify an Italian national culture one has to start from its regional cultures. He wrote splendid poetry in Friulian. Calvino, on the other hand, said that one had to start at the universal level in order to reach the regional. I agree with Pasolini, and that is the reason I claim that an Italian culture outside of Italy does exist. If what I told you is true, we have to make an effort to give an identity, a credibility, to this regional Italian-Canadian culture. It's a simple concept, but making it understood is very difficult.

A.M.: *And yet the universities, which here in Canada have first-class departments of Italian Studies, should be open to these concepts.*

A.D.: Universities are still studying Italy through Dante or the Renaissance. A classical vision, but lacking any living culture. How can an eighteen- or twenty-year old understand modern Italy by studying Dante or the Renaissance? I would find a way around it. I would arrive at Dante, the Renaissance, Verga, even Pasolini and Morante, through the best Italian-Canadian writers, those who have reached an awareness of the modern Italian identity. By "modern," I mean some situation having the past as cultural heritage, but keeping your eyes on the present and future. There are some who do this, and not just a few.

In Pasquale Verdicchio's poetry, for instance, you can find Dante and classical Italian culture; being a contemporary, therefore he can be understood and act as a go-between for he who is and what is behind him. Something else, very important in my opinion, can be deduced from this: Italian culture, for its specificity and sheer size, is contradictory, provocative, multi-faceted, paradoxical, European. We Italians, we Europeans, have defined culture as the synthesis of opposites. These things were understood in Quebec because they practiced them, trying to give specificity to their cultural identity. That's why being authentically Italian is easier in Montreal than in Toronto.

A.M.: *That's strange, because multiculturalism . . .*

A.D.: I'll tell you my opinion, defying popular opinion. Multiculturalism, as a matter of fact, does not exist. Canadian multiculturalism, when all is said and done, only accepts anglophones and francophones.

A.M.: *This looks like a paradox.*

A.D.: Quebec is not multicultural, but it's open; whereas Ontario pretends to be multicultural but it's closed. People in Ontario speak English, like in most of Canada, yet they are not part of British culture. Many act as though they were British, but they are not. Such an attitude entails unacceptable closures and absolute certainties. Doubt, elasticity, and willingness to understand other cultures do not operate here. That's why I feel that Trudeau's multiculturalism was never put into practice.

If one agrees with what I just said, the conclusion can only be that the dominant culture has two prevailing aspects. First, for Anglo-Saxon Canadians culture is a business and must give immediate returns, although the rhythm of the economy does not often coincide with that of culture. Second, it is unacceptable that a non-Anglo-Saxon, an Italian in our case, can ever be successful on his or her own terms. Non-British people find that someone has barred the doors. Only those authors who abjure their culture will be received with open arms. I have never accepted this sort of cultural blackmail, and therefore am paying the consequences.

A.M.: *What consequences?*

A.D.: Let me tell you a story. At the beginning when I believed in multiculturalism I asked one of the Councils for the Arts to recognize the works of authors, having Italian names, but born here. My request was rejected because, they said, these authors are not considered Canadian. I even sent back the photocopies of their passports to prove to them that they were indeed Canadian. I was told in the end that the writers might be Canadians, but their books were not. Works having an Italian inspiration did not have a Canadian content. The result: no grant. Do you understand why I say that Canada is bicultural at best, and multiculturalism does not really exist? From that moment on, I refuse to publish works that propose assimilation to Canada's dominant cultures.

A.M.: *In your words, Quebec would seem the ideal place for producing culture. But you left Montreal and moved to Toronto. How can you explain this apparently contradictory decision?*

A.D.: With two reasons. One is of a personal nature: my daughter was born in Toronto and I will stay here until she is able to choose where she wants to live. The other one is political: in 1991, I broke with the Parti Quebecois and some intellectuals. I always had, and always proclaimed, a pluricultural vision of Canadian society. Politicians in Quebec want a supremacy of a francophone culture, and this, although a little more open than the anglophone one, also shows appalling closures. Some writers said that I had been brainwashed by Trudeau. The fact of the matter is that Trudeau was not for pluriculturalism. He believed in interculturalism, where the "other" is required to embrace one of the dominant cultures. In general I broke with the establishment, which is never candid and everywhere shares the same characteristics.

A.M.: *Let me go back to my initial question. In Canada, given the massive presence of Italians who could be said to be Italy's twenty-first region, what exists of the authentically Italian beyond the façade?*

A.D.: There's an Italian-Canadian identity, under the ashes of the stereotypes, which we are identified by and which we ourselves often resort to. These commonplaces range from nostalgia to a purely classical vision of Italian culture, and they are to be found both in the parties of local Italian clubs and in university classes.

If we brush those ashes away, we'll find that a high-quality Italian-Canadian culture and artistic production do exist. We have yet taken notice of them. It is an insult to Italian-Canadian artists that many should still be suffering in isolation and poverty when they could have been given jobs in colleges and universities, like the Quebecois do with their artists. As far as Italy is concerned, it must accept that Italian literature abroad cannot be in Italian, because the cultural commonwealth we created is as wide as the world, and the world does not necessarily speak Italian. Italic culture, because of its specificity, deserves citizenship all over the world. I proclaim equal dignity for it. Even if this means losing grants from the federal and provincial governments.

Making Italian a Living Language

There is much talk on the Italian language these days. This is good news. And I am also glad that someone actually pulled out figures regarding which languages are projected to survive and which are are not. According to UNESCO, it is estimated that a language needs a minimum of 150 million people for it to survive. If we go by this figure, we have to admit that the Italian language is in crisis.

There are approximately 63 million speakers of Italian in the world today. Italian can therefore be compared to Javanese (61 million), Vietnamese (61 million), Wu (the language of Shanghai, 64 million), and Cantonese (the language of some parts of mainland China and Hong Kong, 65 million). Italian, however, is far from attaining the same cultural penetration as Mandarin (907 million), English (456 million), Hindi (383 million), Spanish (362 million), Portuguese (177 million), French (123 million), or German (119 million).

Linguists estimate that there are roughly five thousand distinct languages in the world today. Half of these are expected to die in the coming decades. This is sad news. Yet there is something that can be done in the case of Italian. Not that Italian will ever attain the scope of, say, Portuguese, simply because Italy never had colonies (other than Ethiopia and Somalia, for a brief period in the 1920-40s). Nor is there a country that helps Italy in the same way that Brazil helps Portugal, or Quebec helps France.

Unlike the French, Italians do not have a *francophonie (francofonia)* as a base for achieving unity. A famous living poet from Italy has lamented that it is absurd to be writing in a dying language. As true as this may seem to be, surely we can transmit something of the Italian language to our children. History is proof that Italian culture has survived, even though it is not preserved solely in the Italian language.

As honorable as it is to teach Dante and Boccaccio to young men and women, I wonder if it would not be better, at present, to initiate them into the Italian language in a different way. It is not Dante that keeps me speaking Italian to my daughter. It is the everyday chores I am forced to do. Instead of unearthing the dead in order to attract the young, why not show the young (and not so young) a Canadian culture in Italian? There are books by Canadians (English and French) that have been translated into Italian. There are Canadian films translated into Italian. Then there is all the American stuff we see every night on TV, translated into Italian. Why not teach Italian through using these works of contemporary culture, translated into Italian? This would, for one, enable the elderly to understand what they can't understand on TV, and would also help the young see the world through the filter of the Italian language.

This is the wager. Professors and TV producers should show us the reality that is immediately available to us, and this actuality will make Italian appear real and

necessary to us. As long as Italian is a foreign phenomenon, it will always remain distant from our lives; Italian will be something that belongs only to Italy, not to
the others living abroad.

Italians in Canada are in a very similar situation to
the Quebecois. The difference is that the Quebecois
were cautious enough to come up with legal tools that
have kept their language alive. They watch *Seinfeld* in
French. This may seem strange to Torontonians, but it
isn't to my parents in Montreal. This sort of exercise
keeps the French language alive, makes French a living
and pulsating thing. It's real, not something that belongs
to France.

There is not enough Italian material (besides com-
mercials) available to us. Italian should be readily available here and not only from Italy.

As T.S. Eliot once wrote, translation is the barometer of a healthy culture. There is simply not enough
translation going on in the Italian language. If Carole
David, Barry Callaghan, or Nino Ricci were taught in
Italian, we would understand our country in a different
way. Umberto Eco or Mario Luzi alone cannot keep
the Italian language alive. A language that only exports
will ultimately bring death to itself. For the Italian language to survive it must import foreign products into
its world.

The Impracticability of Having
One Major Center

I am writing this text listening to *Oh What a Feeling,* a compilation of Canadian music that came out in 1996, produced by the Canadian Academy of Recording Arts and Sciences – a long-awaited project that gives the listener a sense of what is being done musically in English Canada.

But what about the other Canada? Where is French Canada in the history of Canadian rock?

There exists a discriminatory attitude towards French music that I would like to see come to an end. There is no excuse for this sort of cultural blindness. Canada is not only English-speaking. To say it is, is a deliberate attack on what makes this country different from Britain, France, and the U.S.A.

As a writer it is my job to work towards uprooting this cultural intransigence. But I don't have the financial resources. The only way to crack the wall of cultural centripetalism is to open the minds of politicians and the business people who are responsible for keeping this country divided into two opposing forces. The division of this country is intentional – a way of preventing the one side from encroaching onto the territory controlled by the other.

Ethnic cultures, if they are to flourish, must break down this wall of the Great Divide. Without the dismantling of this financial, cultural, and political wall, ethnic communities will have to split themselves and work simultaneously in both sides.

This division of ethnic communities, too, is intentional. Ethnic communities, once divided, pose no serious threat to the lucrative shrines on either side of the cultural wall. We have few options, if any at all. The job is to find ways of uniting our different centers in the midst of independence and separateness.

If the Italian community wants to create a center for its cultural survival it will have to do so by working from various centers located in disparate parts of the country. There is no other way that the Italian community will be able to reach beyond the current cultural divide and act as a unified group.

The dissimilarities are too great. You can't ask the Left to create a coalition with the Right. There are French-speaking Italians (and there will be more of these as the Italian community embraces Quebec's cultural project) who will have no desire to deal with, say, the Toronto center.

And I am not certain that Italian Canadians from other parts of English Canada will accept Toronto as the only center for things Italic. Whether Italian Canadians like it or not, we will have to stop dreaming of ever having a single center that will act as an umbrella for all Italian Canadians. This is neither desirable nor practical.

Geographical distances (and regional differences) make a single center impractical. Nepotism and cultural biases make a single center undesirable. To limit Italian-Canadian culture to the university would be detrimental to the survival of difference. There simply are not enough free writers and intellectuals in our universities to guarantee Italic communities in this country diversity and openness, and to leave cultural projects to business people is to smother freedom of choice.

The Italic communities of Canada and North America, or for that matter across the world, are, generally speaking, not at all synchronized by the cultural effervescence (ethnic or not) on their respective territories. Culture is what is left over when banks close their doors.

We have to be able to spend money blindly; that is, business people must take risks. They must be able to hand over their hard-earned money to men and women with ideas. They must be willing, not to only forfeit the power their money has given them, but accept the consequences of losing both that power and the money. In other words, business people have to be generous, extremely generous.

All this squabbling over one centripetal center is not a sign of munificence. In fact, it seems to demonstrate how profoundly discourteous we, as members of a cultural community, still are to one another. No one takes what the others do seriously.

I do not wish to throw a hammer in the spokes of cultural management. I feel that we have not yet come to grips with what is truly at stake when people use semantically charged terms such as Italian, Canadian, English Canadian, American Canadian, French Canadian, Quebecois. Many writers have written extensively on these issues. Why not consult them? If we don't it is probably because we think writers are a trifle in the scheme of real issues. If writers are frivolous, then what kind of culture are we wrangling about?

The role of the university is to teach. The role of business is to administer financial resources. The role of artists is to create. It would be great if all three communities could co-habit. It won't happen. The best solution would be to encourage business to be generous to both the university and the artist; have the university teach what the artist creates; remind the artist to be thankful to both the university and business, because without them, he/she would not exist.

Culture comes alive only if we, its members, take ourselves seriously. Cultural centers already exist. They might not be what cultural dictators dream of, but they are here, functioning in their own modest way. Culture is a very fragile gift we give themselves. Talking about ways of controlling culture as a colonial by-product is a waste of time. Canada is not England. Canada is not France. Why pretend Canada can be Italy?

A Conversation
Interview with Jennifer Sipos

Jennifer Sipos: *You and I are just kind of having a conversation. I'm just going to adjust the camera a little bit.*

Antonio D'Alfonso: I don't have any makeup.

J.S.: *You don't have any makeup? That's so frustrating, I hate that. Anyway, the first question I want to ask you . . .*

A.D.: Why don't you turn that thing so it's easier for you? There we are.

J.S.: *You're so smart.*

A.D.: I have one of those cameras.

J.S.: *Oh, really? What do you use it for?*

A.D.: Interviews as well.

J.S.: *Do you really?*

A.D.: Yes.

J.S.: *Is that part of research for your screen writing, or . . .*

A.D.: No, no, no. As a writer – I'm a frustrated filmmaker. But I use it mostly to archive writers.

J.S.: *Oh really?*

A.D.: I have met so many great writers in my life and now they are dead and gone and I regret not filming them. I should have filmed them in 16 mm; it would have been more appropriate. You know when you are in the arts, unfortunately in this country you can't do different types of jobs. If you are a writer you can't be a filmmaker; if you are a filmmaker you can't be a playwright; if you are a playwright you can't be a painter.

J.S.: *Oh, don't tell me that. Is that really true?*

A.D.: Absolutely. It is one thing to be told that; it is another thing to experience elimination by yourself. Eventually time just is not enough. There's not enough time to do everything. And that is how I feel now. I like music, film, photography, and writing. Those are my big daggers. So when I was a filmmaker I did not meet writers and I should have, and when I started meeting writers they told me to stop filmmaking. After being in the literary milieu for thirty years, I'm now allowed to photograph writers. They would not have let me do that before. Writers are very fussy about who photographs them.

J.S.: *I'm sure you will enjoy going back over what you have captured at a later date.*

A.D.: At a later date . . . if I ever get there.

J.S.: *How did you get started in the business?*

A.D.: I started as . . . a scientist. I got into biology and I got my Masters in Science.

J.S.: *And was that here in Canada?*

A.D.: In Montreal. I'm from Montreal. From biology I got into theatre as an actor. I'm a lousy actor. I might be a better on screen, but on stage I was horrendous.

J.S.: *Really?*

A.D.: Yes. By acting in short films I got curious about being behind the camera. I shot two films as a B.A. student and one longer film independently. Film led me away from science for a while. I ran back to science when I studied linguistics and semiology and applied that methodology to film.

J.S.: *Was this part of a thesis that you did?*

A.D.: I did a thesis on Robert Bresson. I analyzed *Mouchette* using the approach of a structural theorist. That was back in the early 1970s. There was no one in Canada who was qualified enough to take my thesis on, so I had to go see a structural architect. A linguist. He said, "Okay, I'm not very good in film but I'll help you along with structural analysis." And that led me to analyzing film.

J.S.: *What theorists did you use then when you were doing . . . ?*

A.D.: Roland Barthes, Christian Metz and A.J. Greimas. The trinity.

J.S.: *I'm using Barthes right now.*

A.D.: What are you reading?

J.S.: *I'm reading* Mythologies.

A.D.: Use *S/Z.*, because *Mythologies* is cute, but *S/Z* is . . .

J.S.: *S/Z?*

A.D.: *S/Z*. What he does is analyze a story by Balzac, *Sarrasine* – he just stops reading and says, "Look what's happening here." At first, the analysis feels weird, you want to shout, "How dare you stop a sentence here." But Barthes doesn't care. He says, "Let's analyze this sentence and see where it goes." He pulls it out of context and off he goes. You see what he is trying to do and you say, "Okay." And he says, "Look there's one code at work here, another code there, and another code here." He moves and cuts another sentence. He asks, "So what's happening here? Look, the same codes apply." Finally he gets to the end of the story and everything about the story turns out to be limited to about seven codes. That's incredible, because one would think that cutting up a story into so many little segments would yield an infinite number of meanings. But that is not what happens. Everything anywhere in one story is limited by the story itself. I decided to apply a similar methodology to *Mouchette,* a disturbing film I love. Stopping the film anywhere to analyze what is happening. I used Metz's syntagms for the segments and went on from there. What is the image telling you? What is the sound telling you? What is the voice telling you? What is the director telling you? Surprisingly enough, meaning is quite limited.

J.S.: *You were looking for patterns in these things?*

A.D.: That's the idea. The motor behind structuralism is that you try to illegally create codes. "Illegally" because most art forms aren't supposed to be codified or codifiable. Architecture is, maybe language is, poetry too, but films are not. Film artists have no language to work from and so end up inventing their own language each time. Learning this came as a great disappointment. Because here is a great art that is in the hands of a minority and unfortunately we are being told the same stories over and over again, as great as they are or as bad as they are. In the hands of great filmmakers, film can truly expand minds – precisely because there are no rules; film is an art without limits. It is limitless.

J.S.: *If it is a limitless art, how is it then in teaching you use a very structured formula, and teach your students to reach people through a very formulaic system? That's one of the things that's been most fascinating for the group, in terms of*

learning about how to structure a film and how to set it up.
Maybe you can talk a little bit about your formula and some
of the people who influenced you.

A.D.: I really believe in what Robert Bresson teaches us about film. Again, Robert Bresson. I always go back
to him. There are few people I always go back to:
Robert Bresson and Jean-Luc Godard. Bresson says that
the only way for you to be free is by working in a very
rigid system. And that is something that has always fascinated me. As a writer I am very rigid myself. I refuse
to let myself go when I write. I do, I mean I have let
myself go, I go crazy at times, but always within bounds.
When I constrain myself basically to four or five lines,
I'm forced to truly analyze (1) what is happening on the
surface, and (2) what words will I use. I also have to be
aware of the emotions I'm transmitting. That is what I
find fascinating about art: restrictions, in fact, are
extremely liberating.

J.S.: *Very interesting. How does that work? How is it for*
you?

A.D.: Humanity keeps telling the same story. You
learn that when you read *Mythologies*. We keep on
telling the same stories. Basically, we know what stories
we are telling and we should know how to tell these
stories. It is interesting to teach future writers how
these stories are told. And encourage them to work in
a structure. It is a false conception that certain structures prevent you from liberating yourself. The problem
is that we are not exposed to different types of realities,
we are not exposed to different types of filmmaking.
Different poems by poets from different realities. And so

you come back and say, "Well, I want to write a sonnet that has to rhyme A, B, C." Big deal, that bothers me. I'm not a formalist. I believe in structure, but I do not believe in formalism. Structure is the opposite of formalism. People say to me, I'm a structuralist therefore I believe in form. I am anti-form because forms are boring. Forms are backwards, I do not believe in the type of prison-structures that we, as a human species, have invented for ourselves, unconsciously or consciously. What fascinates me about all art forms is structure. So if I tell a student, "Oh, look what's happened in the first ten minutes in the film," it is because I want to encourage consciousness about how the story is about to develop. Whether you watch a film by Godard or one by Spielberg, something inevitably occurs at about the ten-minute point. My job as a teacher is to remind you: "Look what's happening here. Look what happens at twenty minutes. Look what happens at thirty minutes. And then again at forty-five minutes." There is a semantic structure we are following. People who are not structuralists will come up with similar theories, about what happens at thirty minutes, but they do not truly analyze what is happening on a deeper level – what is semantically happening at that precise moment. How do we get to that deeper meaning? I believe it is mathematical. Meaning works like a mathematical equation. A plus B equals C. And whether you like it or not, that is where you have to go. If you introduce elements A and B, then you have no choice but to go towards C. If you do not go towards C, you are going to fail. And you will fail. You might be upset and say, "I don't want C, I want D." Then I will tell you, "Go for D. Try it." But if D does not work, you will know the reason why. Things in art happen because things have to happen there and then. There are no two ways about it. This sort of reasoning intrigues me.

The call for structure has nothing to do with form. Form imposes pre-established answers; structure can only suggest the equation that will lead to a wider range of possible solutions. I am anti-formula. I do not want to teach artistic formulae. All I am trying to do is teach the awareness of how structures function. A form is something that we invent, "That's how a sonnet must be written. That's how a short story must be written." But the fact of the matter is that there are no laws as to how a sonnet must be written. There is something that happens on line two, and that is intriguing. Tell the mind to go to that precise point, and let it play around with invention.

J.S.: *You said somewhere that you don't believe in psychology.*

A.D.: That's right.

J.S.: *Can you talk a little bit about that? And how that plays into or does not play into your process when you write?*

A.D.: I do not believe in psychology. Psychology is not psychiatry, it is not psychoanalysis. Psychoanalysis again works with structures. What is psychology? Are you trying to tell me something or am I trying to tell myself something: "Oh yeah, if you bang the door, I'll be upset." Of course I will be upset. I told you I would be upset if you banged the door. Why shouldn't I be upset? It might have taken me forty years to admit it that if you walk out of a room and bang the door you'll make me upset. Where does that leave me, you, the door? What is fascinating about psychoanalysis is that what is happening is taken as a fact. What does the door mean? Where does that door lead you and how far back can you go with that door? What type of structure can be created that bridges me, you, and the door? This is the unconscious structure you have created for yourself at that moment. Your job is to figure out why you created that particular structure.

Why are you doing *that* to yourself? I am an emotional being but emotions are very complex, and I do not think that you can rely on emotions to create. After I got divorced, I sat down and wrote an emotional poem. It was pure crap. Better stuff followed when I became totally sober.

Later I was commissioned to write about the experience and the later poem is a better poem than the one I wrote when I was emotionally sick. What you produce with the emotional part of your mind creates a much more lasting experience than what you produce when it is the hurting brain of your heart that speaks. Emotions aren't really important when it comes to creativity. What is important is to know where you are going. That is fundamental. Where are you going and why you are going there? Those ideas command structures that you create yourself based on your experience. I'm very exacting on this point. I always ask writers, "Why do you want to do this? Why are you writing this way? Why have you chosen this path?" Not because a character needs to *feel* this particular emotion. No character has to feel anything in particular. He needs to act, and it is in action performed at the proper moment that emotion is released. Not the other way around. Bresson would say: Have no emotion, act mechanically and let things follow.

J.S.: *And now that you have this formula* . . .

A.D.: Not formula, structure.

J.S.: *Not formula, structure. Now that you have this working structure, how does your process improve or grow? Because your structure is working so well for you and it's obviously benefitting other people too. How do you make it better? How does your next script become better?*

A.D.: Things constantly change. You are constantly faced with a story to tell. The story has to go in a particular direction, and you know that a direction must be taken at this precise moment in the story. You start thinking: What should happen here? And what is the most fascinating door to open?

You know something has to happen at thirty minutes, on page thirty, but fear sets in. Knowing something has to happen, you sit down and say, "Let me take this direction." And everybody around you is pointing in the same direction. That direction, however easy, rarely offers the proper solution to your riddle. Because your answer will never be found at the end of that road. Whenever you believe you have found an easy answer, it is your duty to go against that solution and aim in the opposite direction. If the easy solution lies on the right, then go left. If it is on the left, go right. If a rhyme is needed, don't put the rhyme there. Form, psychology will impose an answer.

Structure is a prison that says you can't go outside, yes, but unlike form, where a prison is a four-walled room, structure offers you a room that need not be a square or a rectangle. The prison might be, instead, a pentagon, a hexagon, an octagon. Form limits you, structure makes art limitless. The work will be constantly changing and you, as an artist, will be constantly faced with the task of finding new solutions for every new problem that appears before you.

I'm always impressed by how the little prison that I have created for myself enables me to get out of the pitfalls I have created in interesting ways. This does not mean that what I do will be popular or successful. The fact that I work and have come up with a sonnet or a script or a song does not necessarily mean that what I did is going to be a great thing. Success is not something I strive for. The creative process is what is essential to me. I'm glad I have done what I did.

What counts, is the *production* of things, not the things in themselves. Eventually those things add up and there will be a system that will manifest itself. People might say, "I like what Jennifer does," "I hate that one book Jennifer wrote," but in the end if what Jennifer produces is consistent, her work will reflect a system that will be uniquely Jennifer's. What counts is to have people say, "I like the artist she *is.*" Sadly, the world of art does not work this way. People today are fanatically obsessed with success. One does things to be successful, and glorification of success is damaging to the mind.

J.S.: *I think so too.*

A.D.: Not only damaging to the mind but damaging to society as a whole. When I say I believe in structure, that structure is also something that I have to fight against. Where and how far can I push music, so that the twelve-tone system in music becomes thirteen? All of a sudden, this is no longer a need for A, B, C. What is called for becomes a totally diverse thing. It is J. "But J doesn't exist in the do-re-mi system!" the critics scream.

When a composer invents or introduces a letter like J or K into the musical system, how does such an element modify the scale of things musical? The composer is still respecting the scale but he has lifted the scale a notch, or lowered it. If he goes there, it's like being in between two notes. That is what I like about the idea of lying at the opposite side of the spectrum of success. Once you have written a script, your job is to say, "Sit down, friend, and see where we can really tighten it up."

J.S.: *Does that process ever end?*

A.D.: Never.

J.S.: *It never ends?*

A.D.: Never.

J.S.: *Does it only end at the request of somebody else? When the filmmaker or the person who is buying the script sets a deadline, and you finally say, "Okay, I have to let this go."*

A.D.: Absolutely. Look at the great minds, these are people who on their death beds were still tightening up a line or fixing up an image on works they had produced when they were younger. One is constantly going back to his own past and saying, "This is not really what I wanted to do. I think I know what I want to do now." One can produce a film today with less money. Adding a fade-out, for example, cost a fortune in the 1960s. Today, with the press of a button on your camera you get a perfect fade-out. Art is a process, it is not about finished products like loaves of bread or pairs of shoes.

J.S.: *What do you do when you're not teaching? Do you write full-time?*

A.D.: I'm a writer and a publisher. So I deal with artists, writers, photographers, graphic artists, typographers, and printers on a daily basis. I have been continually dealing with different people who have different ideas about different things since the age of twenty-five. I have been in the publishing business for twenty-five years, and a writer for thirty years. My publishing house works in a very structured way too. Being totally chaotic, I try very hard to be organized. *[Laughter.]*

J.S.: *So does that make you a bit of a perfectionist as well?*

A.D.: Of course. One has to be.

J.S.: *To get what you want? To be satisfied, is that what you mean?*

A.D.: You are the best judge. You are steadily trying to find something you will be happy with. It is not like lovemaking. Lovemaking is sometimes good, sometimes not so good. You can't be so indulgent with writing. Writing has to be good; when you write a poem you want it to be good. To be good in your eyes. Not successful, simply good. If a poem fails, if everything I do is a failure, then I can say that I have failed. If I fail, I have to learn to accept my own failure. I tell people I have made three films that are all very bad. So what? I still love them. I know exactly where they went wrong. I know why they are bad. Still, those films are very present in my mind, they are part of my growth process.

J.S.: *How long did it take you to adopt this sort of mind-set, this attitude?*

A.D.: I was lucky enough to have had it grow in me. It began at the age of fourteen. When I was a younger man I tried to follow a certain political ideology, you know, being a Marxist and a left winger. But Marx did not give me what I was looking for. That came through reading the right authors, people like Gurdjieff. The "Fourth Way" system. It made sense. One plus one does not equal two, it equals four. The plus sign and the equal sign mean something in that equation. Addition adds something to the elements. Marx taught us one plus one equals three; his ideas were based on principles of the thesis, antithesis, and synthesis. But he did not realize that the three elements themselves made up a fourth one. And that fourth element, it was Gurdjieff who taught me that. Though I'm not a follower of Gurdjieff, I respect his thought. His ideas paved the way to my rediscovery of structuralism, which has played an important part in my way of seeing things artistic. But all of this took a long time to mature.

When you are analyzing a work you never think that ideas of this kind can actually help you on the creative side. Never. Arthur Rimbaud stopped writing before he was twenty. Yet that young man changed the whole history of French literature. Totally, and with a couple of pages. When I was growing up I told myself that I wanted to be like Rimbaud. It did not happen. It's not going to happen. Such phenomena happen once in the entire lifetime of humanity (Mozart, Charlie Parker). I told myself to be more modest, that I was not going to change mankind in any way. All I can do is make sure that I am happy with what I do. One big obstacle has been imposed on us all: the older we get, the less time we have to achieve the goals we have set out for ourselves. When one is young, one can, if well-connected, produce a lot of material. I mean one can produce hundreds of books. Most of that stuff will critically peter out. Only the best, the really good works will remain. Much of my creativity went into writing letters. Private things that will never see the light of day. I no longer keep a diary. I used to keep a diary but it is not very good. It is too intellectual, not down to earth. I should have recorded what I saw, not what I felt. Most of my anger, most of my emotional turmoil, my fuck-ups get expressed in the letters I send people. And all my passion . . .

J.S.: *Do you actually send those letters to people?*

A.D.: Of course.

J.S.: *Part of your self-reflective process happens in your descriptions to other people.*

A.D.: That's right. And they're very selfish letters most of the time . . .

J.S.: *Yes, you're talking about your . . .*

A.D.: Those emotions have to go out somewhere.

J.S.: *Oh God.*

A.D.: At least for me that's true. Since my writing is so cold, all that bullshit boiling inside of me has to come out somewhere . . . and for me it's in my letters. The people who read them can confidently say, "Oh, look at him: he did have a soul after all, he's not some cold bastard."

J.S.: *Oh my gosh, that's funny. I'm looking to connect the dots for my own interest and sort of . . .*

A.D.: Study another culture. Trust me.

J.S.: *I'm going to Asia in . . .*

A.D.: You have to learn another culture.

J.S.: *You think so?*

A.D.: Because one's own culture, when I say culture, it doesn't matter where one is from, is limiting. There are six million people in this city and at 6:30 pm Toronto disappears. It is a vacant parking lot. It's boring. I went to a restaurant the other day, 9:30 pm was its last service for a meal. I couldn't believe it.

In Montreal we go to restaurants at 10:30 pm. People rush home here. What would be great, would be to prevent people from going home. No matter where your home is, the idea is to encourage people to stick around and eat and drink and talk with one another.

One's home is a rectangular prison. Montreal writer John Buell wrote in one of his novels that home is where you hang yourself. You're going to find the answers to your questions elsewhere. Because that elsewhere has lived the same experiences you have, but has resolved your problems in a different way and with different solutions. For a thousand and one reasons.

The good thing about Canada is that you do not have to travel far to meet another culture. You don't have to go to Asia, as you said, Asia is next door. It does not matter where you go, solutions can be found wherever there is difference.

I grew up as an Italian kid who went to English school, but it was when I started to live as a French-speaking Quebecois that my life found its meaning. Living with the Quebecois changed my life. I work in French even though I speak with an accent.

J.S.: *I thought you were a francophone.*

A.D.: Yes, I am, but I'm also an anglophone. I began my French experience at the age of fourteen. I'm Italian. Some people call me a francophone but I'm Italian, my daughter is Italian. I eat Italian, minus the meat. Yet I never felt that the Italian culture had all the answers to the questions that were popping up in my mind. Obviously I found some solutions within my Italian culture, yet not all the solutions the Italian culture offers me are of interest to me. I have to go elsewhere for certain answers, and the French culture offers different solutions to several of my problems.

J.S.: *That's really interesting. My sister just came back from Barcelona. She lived there for a year and she just went back for a couple of weeks, and I think she would say what you are saying about French culture about the Spanish culture.*

A.D.: A friend of mine who is French fell in love with a Muslim Indonesian and has adopted that culture because it gives him the things he is looking for. He lives in Jakarta. Another friend, Italian-born but who lived in Montreal for thirty years, went back to Italy with his dual citizenship. One day he decided to tear up his Italian passport and become a full-fledged Canadian. He no longer cares about being Italian, even if he lives in Bologna, he doesn't want to be part of that culture. He considers himself a Canadian. The idea is that we all live in some sort of cultural prison, might as well make it a prison that is larger than a prison with four walls.

Virtual Ethnics

1

Ethnicity is not going to die. Ethnicity has always been the enemy of national cultures. In America (North and South) where there is no national culture, ethnicity should not be viewed as an enemy but as its very essence.

Ethnicity is the vision of the world conceived as a conglomeration of ethnic communities. The ethnic community is a group of autonomous individuals who share, to quote the U.S. sociologist Nathan Glazer, "a common history and experience and is defined by descent, real or mythical."

2

The difference between ethnicity and nationalism is important to understand. Ethnics are not necessarily bound by territory. They are groundless. They can be anywhere, living in a culture that did not arise out of the land they are living and working in.

Nationalism, however, is ethnicity reduced to territorial identity. Nationalism is tribal in spirit.

There are two traditional ways to identify an individual: according to *jus solis* – whereby identity is derived from one's place of birth; *jus sanguinis* – whereby identity is based on blood relationship.

But how does one identify, say, an Lithuanian in Toronto, who was not born in Lithuania? And what about the Portuguese citizen who is not born of Portuguese parents? Can we call the person born outside of Italy and whose parents were not themselves born in Italy Italian, even if he or she calls himself or herself Italian?

3

What is identity? The sum of elements which mysteriously make me the individual that I am. Identity, in my opinion, must necessarily include the ethnic.

Identity, because it is ethnic, has a strong odor. Identity *stinks.* This is why ethnicity is not a popular term in the world today, not in America, not in Europe, not in Asia, not in Africa. National cultures do everything they can to bulldoze ethnicity out of existence. But ethnicity without a territory has always existed and will always exist.

4

Awareness of self is, however, never a simple task. It can literally tear you apart. But so can the absence of self-awareness. When awareness of self sets in, a person can no longer act irresponsibly. But how does one become aware of one's culture? There are two ways: either by letting go of one culture and embracing a second culture; or by pulling one's culture to different levels of meaning. Culture is not a stagnant thing. It is in constant flux, moving everywhere, contracting, expanding, taking new shapes and sizes.

5

To base one's identity on a culture in America ultimately means that you will have to deal with ethnic
questions. You will have to define yourself, not only by
territory, but by some different parameters as well. I
don't know what these parameters are. My job is to
make sure that ethnic identity does not get imprisoned
by ideas of national territory, blood, religion and, in
many cases, language.

6

My struggle with Quebec was never over the separatist
issue, since I still think that Quebec has more to gain by
freeing itself from Canada. It is so different from the rest
of the country – its laws, its language, its culture – it
might as well become an independent country. My beef
against Quebec is its territorial nationalism. Quebec's
identity is more than language. It possesses a unique
world view. Since the majority of French-speaking
Canadians who share this particular world view are
located in one specific territory, it is natural for them to
speak of separatism. I would have preferred that they
approach the question of identity as ethnics, and this
they will never do. Nor will the British Canadians.

This is the major problem with our country. If the
founding peoples of Canada refuse to be considered
ethnics, then they are forcing the rest of the population
into third-class citizenry. (First-class being French in
Quebec and British in Canada; and second-class being
French in Canada and English in Quebec.)

7

Aterritorial identity stands at the opposite pole of national identity. National identity imposes a *modus operandi* (manner of doing things) that does not tolerate difference. Nations, like France, Italy, Britain, Germany, incorporate minority groups gradually but surely, and then swallow them up.

Complete assimilation is the overt program of all nations. Strangers are expected to be absorbed by the larger community. If they are not, they will be ostracized and asked to leave. Immigration, as is clear by now, is the most serious problem of European nation-states. Each nation has one motto: a single identity in a single nation.

8

America is not Europe. America, whether it is Canada, the U.S.A., Brazil, Mexico, or Argentina, is made up of two continents, many countries, many minority communities. America is made up of countries of many collectivities, races, religions. Even the inter-mixed groups are without a nation in America. All are without a ground or a territory they can claim as their own.

There are no cultural communities in the Americas that can ever claim a piece of land and call for separation. I am sure that American cultural minorities wouldn't separate even if the chance to claim a territory were given them. It is not part of the American psyche. Even the Native notion of territory is one without borders.

9

Identity in America is not based on territory. Identity emerges from consciousness, as it happens in the domain of religious experience, where one can be a born again Christian. The same is true of cultural awareness. Cultural awareness is necessarily a rediscovering, a rebirth to a new identity. Ethnic identity is identity to the power of two. This is why I believe that conscious identity is at the root of American ethnicity, and not place of birth or the blood that runs through my veins.

10

Ethnics are the fishbone in the throat of America. Because there is no group that can rightly claim that America' belongs to it, I believe that ethnicity is not going to fade away in America. It can only grow. But if minorities do not become ethnic communities, the result can only be confusion, pain, torment and, ultimately, suicide.

11

Where does one start? One starts with oneself. One is either asked to assimilate into an ethnic group or not. Even hybrids have to choose which group they will belong to. Hybridity is a process: it is two on the way to becoming one. When people speak of interculturalism in Quebec or multiculturalism in English Canada, this is precisely what is intended. You are permitted to be a hyphenated identity just as long as you shed your particular cultural characteristics and embrace one of the two founding ethnic cultures. In other words, it is all right to be an Italian Canadian just as long as the Italian eventually melts totally into the Canadian side of the hyphen. The problem is that this Canadian side is just as confused as the other side of the equation. Like any other country in America, there is no such thing as a Canadian. It is too vague a term to encompass all that the term implies. To paraphrase the American philosopher Michael Walzer, even if there were such a thing as a Canadian; that is, a Canadian hyphen Canadian, it would be no better or worse than any other hyphenated group. A Canadian Canadian in Canada is just one of the many ethnic groups in the country.

12

Again Michael Walzer, who paraphrases another U.S. thinker, Horace Kallen – the hyphenated identity represents in reality two different things altogether. On the left side, we have the cultural person; on the other side, we have the political citizen. So, in the equation German Canadian, we have on one side the German culture and on the other side the Canadian citizen.

When people say that we have to assimilate, what they are asking us to do is to become citizens without a culture! This is what is asked of minorities here on the American continents. With European nations, assimilation works in a different way. If you assimilate into the nation, the nation offers its own culture in exchange. The process is one of equal standing: one for one.

But when you assimilate in an ethnic country you find yourself with citizenship, but without culture. The assimilated person becomes a simple servant of the state. Is this the hidden agenda of the recent educational reforms (cuts in second-language programs) that governments are trying to sell us? Do they want to rid our children of their cultural traits and turn them into technicians for the state?

13

It is, however, not easy to keep a culture alive on the other side of the hyphen. The individual by himself is helpless. The burden is impossible to carry. Nostalgia and thoughts of a distant paradise lead nowhere but to sadness and despair. For culture to make any sense, for culture to survive, the individual must negotiate with other individuals who share similar cultural and political preoccupations. This is where the idea of a center comes in.

14

What is a center? It is the expanded ghetto. Unfortunately, the ghetto has become a term with negative connotations: a place of confinement, a reserve.

What I mean by ghetto is a deterritorialized (groundless) ghetto: a creative, economic, intellectual, and cultural center of activity. Not a haven for individual nostalgia, but rather cultural consciousness at the political level.

If the cultural side of the hyphen is to have any significance, it must be real and practical. That is why nostalgia, emotional attachment to a motherland, and
private financial success are not practical cultural solutions. These are personal choices, and culture, as personal as it can be, must always be collective for it to have
any political significance. It is this collectivity, once created, that must now develop into a center.

The center can take the form of a place, local and
localized, but it may also not be a place at all. It might
very well be a virtual space, a place that is not anchored
in any one geographical spot. No matter what form the
center takes, what should remain as its main focus is its
health. The center must be healthy and thriving.

15

Ethnicity translocates identity from territory and the
nation to a groundless collectivity. What happens to the
mother nation? This is a sensitive issue that gets many
people agitated. For ethnicity to have any value it must
be able to bridge its culture to similar cultures across
geographical borders. It has to be able to negotiate with
other centers with a common culture first. But for this
to happen the mother nation must be ready to decen-
tralize itself. If the mother nation refuses to do so, the
centers will only be virtual centers with virtual cultural powers. With a centralized Italy, Italians abroad will
only be virtual Italians.

Italy, France, Portugal must accept the fact that they
are no longer the exclusive proprietors of their culture.

They are only one of many holders of their culture.
They must therefore be willing to negotiate with centers outside their borders on an equal standing. If they
refuse to do so, they will have to face their eventual
cultural death. It is known by ethnographers that for
any single culture to survive it needs a pre-established
number of participants. No nation today can survive
without the input of cultural centers abroad.

Yet national cultures have always approached manifestations of their own culture abroad with a good dose
of condescension. National cultures feign superiority
by claiming what belongs to everyone. It is safe to say
that, if national cultures are suffering nowadays, it is in
part their own fault. They act like jealous parents who
prevent their offspring from attaining maturity.

Without this letting go on the part of the mother
nation, without the conscious collectivization of ethnics, no negotiation can ever occur. This is why I
believe that we must want for a culture to survive. It is
in the interest of both the mother nation (as one of
many centers of culture) and ethnic communities (as
centers) to sit at the negotiating table as free and conscious entities intent on forming a commonwealth of
sorts.

16

It is only once negotiating occurs between centers of a
common culture that bridging with other cultures can
begin. The failure to act on the first level will produce
a weak bridge on the second level. If minorities are so

misrepresented in America, it is in great part due to the failure of bridging cultures on these two levels. And this failure has helped American countries to act as European nations, which they are not in essence.

Ethnicity in America never was nor ever will be a passing fad. Ethnicity is here to stay.

Ethnicity cannot be measured by generations. Ethnicity is the foundation of American societies.

It is only when ethnic collectivities overcome the private nostalgia and the rear-view vision of culture of the first-generation immigrants that the serious incorporation of cultures can begin. Only then will ethnic communities in America endow themselves with political powers. Without political representation the individual will never be able to step out of the vapors of a virtual culture.

Markings

Ethnicity as a spiral.

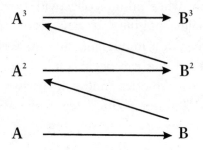

A equals the culture of origin, and B the culture of adoption.

There is no returning to point A, if one has chosen to relocate to B. All movement goes forward from A to A^3, from B to B^3. There is no reversibility in this transit.

Whenever there is a returning to a previous point, it is never to the original state, for A too will have been altered by other factors in the interim.

In the case of reflux, we change the previous state to a negative (-A, -B, -C). This return could be called *nostalgia,* which is the term commonly used to express what, in actual fact, is the quest for lost paradise. The paradox that arises here is that there never existed a paradise in the first place. Nostalgia – because the return trip takes one back to a place that never existed – is a trip to wonderland.

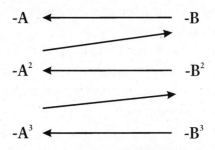

(Clarify possible equivocations which occur when speaking of the homeland.)

There is relocation from point A to point B. In this relocation elements in A will be inevitably transformed by the elements in B.

Traveling from one point to another, in either direction, does not signal any sense of moral progression (evolution) or moral regression (devolution). This transcursion is free of attitude.

2

The elements in A, once transferred, disintegrate in B. These elements may disappear, or they may not, and if they do disappear, it would be a mistake to conclude that they have disappeared forever. There will be instances when certain elements, being only dormant, will, if influenced by a proper drive, reawaken.

Certain elements of A will mix with the elements in B, adopting certain characteristics found in B. We could translate this as A(B), where A is the more important of the two elements found in the compound. We might consider B the stronger element, in which case A becomes less important.

The fusion is never neutral; one element of the compound will always dominate. For example, if B should come to dominate, then we would have B(A).

Four possibilities exist:

A = culture of origin;
B = culture of adoption;
A(B) = culture of origin dominates the culture of adoption;
B(A) = culture of adoption dominates the culture of origin.

If there is be a backward motion, we add a negative sign, whereby the elements of one are less important than the elements of the other.

$$-A(B)$$
$$A(-B)$$
$$B(-A)$$
$$-B(A)$$

What do sets $-A(B)$ and $A(-B)$ mean?

In the case of a person who leaves his/her place of adoption and returns to his/her place of origin, one of the two elements becomes negative.

Either the place of adoption (B) or the place of origin (A) will become the lesser of the two elements. A can never be the same as A of the return. It is false to believe that returning actually means returning. Transmigration can either be a regression (-A) or a progression (A^2). Regression is a downward shift; progression is an upward shift.

We consider this upward movement (progression) essential in the spiral of culture. When one travels back to the point of origin, though not for nostalgic reasons, one brings back both the elements of A and B, thus creating culture to the power of 2, that is A^2. Whatever elements belonged to A, having been altered by elements in B, produce a new entity: A^2.

The merging of elements is so vibrant that moving towards A can only lift the symbiosis to a higher plane.

A is viewed from a higher perspective, and this higher perspective is the beginning of an enhancement of culture, what we call *a pluricultural identity.*

Once this process has begun, returning to origins becomes impossible at every level, since one can no longer free himself/herself of the original elements in A, nor free oneself of the elements of B.

What occurs if standing in point A^2 we look up to B^2? What used to be the culture of adoption (B) has been enhanced by the experience of A^2.

Once one had attained pluricultural consciousness, it is not possible to view culture in a monolithic manner. Persons who have experienced A^2, but now want to live in a B environment, will find themselves raising the cultural status of B to a higher plane as well (B^2)·

What needs to be underscored is that no one world

is preferable to an other. One can be perfectly happy living in A, just as another can be perfectly happy living in B. However, once there is a fusion of different cultural elements from different planes, there can never again be a return to an earlier form. Those who have experienced these pluricultural realities understand that reverse is not possible.

3

Pluriculturalism is this continuous movement from one syncretic culture (A^2) to another (B^2).

In a world of constant shifting from one cultural state to another, one will direct his/her preferences to a particular culture. When this choice has been made, one can never again return to a national culture.

National culture limited to a territory becomes a nonsensical reality for those persons who have experienced associative culture. How can it be otherwise? For people who are able to identify themselves with a global culture no longer limited to a territory, the very notion of territorial culture becomes an aberration. The notion of pluriculturalism rejects the very idea of territorial culture. Pluricultural identity carries us across borders, and leads us to a network of cultural centers without borders.

However, once this jump over territorial culture occurs, one should not expect either the culture of origin or the culture of adoption to remain, in essence, the same. Everything will appear different; everything is different.

When global cultural consciousness emerges, deterritorialized cultures will naturally elevate cultural identity to a higher plane. To confine any one culture to a land and to centralize any culture to one point will bring about the death of that particular culture. The same way as commerce has become increasingly free of boundaries, so must culture be liberated of its boundaries.

Nevertheless, culture is limited. If it weren't, it would not be a culture. Culture is manmade, acquired. It is not like nature, natural. Because culture is learned behavior, we believe that culture may very well occupy similar dimensions and behave in similar ways, in different territories.

If the culture of origin has quite rightly attained a higher level of cultural identification, we may expect this culture of origin, if limited to one territory, to aim at breaking away of its center.

People tend to view culture as being centripetal, leading those at the margins of it towards the center. Modern culture is not centralized. It is because culture has been clamped to a centralized power for so long that we feel the urgent need for a decentralized culture.

Culture is, by essence, complex. It begins somewhere unknown and sluggishly develops into an organic entity that key words, such as *language, religion, territory,* cannot encompass.

What cannot be contained will not be contained. And though in the past culture relied heavily on traditions and habit to keep it alive, we should not expect solutions from the ceremonies of the past to work in the present.

4

The shoemaker sitting beside me on the plane from
Frankfurt asks me what I think of Slovakia separating
from the Czech Republic. I tell him it is for the better.
In a global world, nations are like moth balls, to quote
Nicholas Negroponte, that will turn from solid to gas.
Nations are not the way of the future. We are heading
for enhanced cultures but vanishing nations. This para-
dox, in fact, holds the key of the future.

Cultures will detach themselves from nations, free
themselves and, in doing so, will re-invent themselves.
The walls that incarcerate cultures in one territory will
crumble. Cultures are windows open to the world, no,
not open windows, more like open fields. What is confined will be unconfined. This cultural jump will bring
about difficult consequences at first. People, unable to
accept open territories and what this openness entails,
will ask for artificial barriers that will separate them
from assaulting barbarians.

In a pluricultural world there will be no barbarians,
nor will there be superior peoples. We can no more
shackle a people to a determined piece of land than we
can sanctify a culture because of a nation. With the
spread of a pluricultural consciousness, there will be a
flourishing of cultural contacts that will redefine the
premises on which culture is found.

This unstoppable outburst of contacts will put into
question culture as a centralizing force. Culture will no
longer need a hearth, it will be able to content itself
with various fragments scattered across the world. At
first, this vigorous centrifugal activity will be viewed as

a weakening and dilution of culture, but with time people will discover the liberating energy that a decentralized culture can offer.

This fragmentation will require that we redefine what parameters constitute the cultural individual. This redefinition of culture will call for a new openness of spirit, for any nave that once was known as a mother country will have to forfeit its power in order to initiate commerce with smaller communities spread across the globe. But this breakdown of fulcrum will be, in the long run, a very small price to pay for survival in a world of interconnections.

Those countries that will not let go of their centrifugal force will perish for lack of numbers. In the future, the determining factors of survival will be: (1) the power to conduct commerce with many communities of a similar culture; (2) the willingness to let go of centralized power in order to have a democratic exchange with, at times, smaller communities; (3) the willingness to accommodate the greatest number of communities possible. Failure to open up one's culture will lead to isolation and ultimately to disappearance. New cultural commerce can be translated by elements found in A^3 and B^3, where decentralized cultures will interlock with other decentralized cultures, pushing the entire social fabric to becoming completely decentralized.

5

What I call the Italic culture belongs to a new social contract. Italian culture can no longer be confined to Italy. To continue to believe this is to delude oneself of what Italian culture truly is. Italian culture from Italy is part of a broader spectrum of Italic cultures. But before the final level (A^3) can be attained, the Italian people must admit that they are not the sole proprietors of Italian culture; and that although they might be Italians (from Italy) with an Italian culture (from Italy), they are part of a larger world-wide Italic culture and people.

The Italic culture is far from being achieved. Too many people still believe that Italy is the only place of Italian culture. Too many still want to make the Italian language the one common denominator among the many peoples that make up the Italic culture. This is a dramatic error; there exist many Italics who do not speak, nor need to speak the Italian language.

The Italian language, as beautiful as it is, shines like a fake jewel. It is too provincial for the majority of Italics to want to use in their daily existence. Many have never felt the need nor desire to learn or speak the Italian language and yet none have suffered from absence of the language. Many have been able to maintain their culture, alive and well living abroad, without ever feeling the need to be patriotic or make Italy their homeland. Many, in fact, conduct their lives by working and producing art and literature in another language. The biased view of identifying Italics exclusively with Italy, and insisting that Italics use only the Italian language will ultimately put the Italic in danger.

With the unification of Europe, Italy will probably separate into various distinctive regions. It will be obliged to conduct cultural business in ways it has publicly refused to do. Regionally. Only scientists and scholars, anthropologists and intellectuals will be able to come up with reasons and methods that will assist these regions that, participating in their new borderless cultures, will want to remain together as a country.

A decentralized Italian culture will have to go through a very terrible period of adaptation, hopefully without recourse to violence. Change of this scope is rarely achieved without turmoil. We are speaking of the Italian culture, yet many cultures will go through a similar process of decentralization and redefinition.

6

There are two branches of Italic culture: one from Italy and the other from outside Italy, each expressing itself in a distinct language: Italian, Italian dialects (including dialects formed from the mixing of non-Italian languages), English, French, German, Spanish, Portuguese, and other languages.

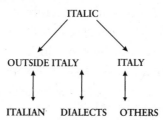

7

Some decide to cross over to B, abandoning A forever. Everyone is free to choose. They should be aware when political powers use them to confuse the others who chose not to stay in B and to cross over to A^2. All are free to choose their destiny, and everyone should become conscious of the responsibilities brought about by his or her decision.

The crossover into a second level need not be final, nor is it a guarantee of success. Certain minority voices are not easily permitted to practice their traditions. We fear the reprisals many cultures will be faced with once they redefine themselves; many will want to eliminate weaker cultures. I do not take it for granted that the Italic voice in English Canada is here to stay. We are ter-rified of what lies in store for all those who think they have it made. Few cultures have ever been accepted into a dominant foreign culture.

The foreign writer, writing in the language of the adopted country, no matter what generation he or she belongs to, will often become a cultural victim. When it is time for the role call, the literary authorities of the dominant culture will simply skip one generation of outlaws and appoint and coronate the next person in line, the one who is willing to embrace the culture in power. The official accolades that the cross-over indi-vidual receives are usually short-lived.

Pascal: *Es-tu moins esclave pour être aimé et flatté de ton maître? Tu as bien du bien, esclave; ton maître te flatte, il te battra tantôt* (158).

8

Heightened cultural identity is a phenomenon free of nationalist sentiments, it is not subservient to territorial demand. Ethnic in spirit, such pluricultural identity cannot alone surmount the limitations assigned by territorial regents. The individual, though independent of the constraints imposed by all cultural compromise, might need collective agreements. Heightened cultural identity is a renewing process of consciousness of the individual's place in society.

Writers across the world are enabling us to study the terms of political entente as never recorded before. For the first time in the history of cultures, we are permitted to view with surprising accuracy what occurs to the first generation, second and third generation, as well as the post-emigrant, who opt for resistance against sameness. Never before have we had, at our disposal, so many sociological tools of cultural analysis. It would be a crime to allow the work of cultural sociologists to vanish in the dust of nationalist indifference and non-cooperation.

Individuals who belong to the network of cultural non-territorial centers should let go of their regional differences (countries of adoption) and begin to reach out to one another and forge links with others who share a similar vision of culture.

We have no false hopes. The same way that Italian history, for instance, reduces its emigration to a single footnote, so does the adoptive dominant culture ignore what it pushes to its margins.

We have no reason to forecast facile solutions, nor do we anticipate that heightened cultural awareness will become an ideology or a new religion. Conscious identity must remain free, and because it is subversive, it should not be exchanged for personal gain. The only merit this vanguard has is that it enables individuals to experience new parameters of identity.

Ethnic culture is no longer at the margins. It has created its own centers, its own source of energy, necessitating a break from the world of stereotypes it has been imprisoned in, at times willingly, willfully.

9

Europe must go through a process of denationalization, and this break from thousands of years of territorial identity will not be easy. It is one thing to strive for European economic unity, it is quite another to waddle towards a nationless culture.

One wonders why culture lags behind economy. Why should culture be less universal than finance? Is it that economy is more intelligent than culture, less xenophobic? Or is it that culture is too greedy? Too regional in spirit?

One result of the breaking loose of national borders will be the outbreak of havoc in regions everywhere. The glue that kept countries together will suddenly let go. Southern Italy will naturally separate from Northern Italy; Bavaria from Northern Germany; Catalan from Spain. This re-emergence of regionalisms will, however, be short-lived. It would be a tragedy to limit pluriculturalism to the sectarian view of the world order. This renewal of old acquaintances must lead to openness and pluriculturalism, and not to walled-in incestuous commerce. The tiniest of regions will rid themselves of their racial and cultural "purity."

Cultural regionalism will have been mutilated to such a degree that we will no longer find it useful. Nor will we find it necessary to find a second body to replace the old one. The skin will be shed, but the ceremony will remain. How the celebration will emerge will be fascinating – for this seeming closing in of regions will not be a movement back to the original state (A) but rather to a second state lying above the original one (A^2). This new regionalism, this birth of centers, will therefore be free of physicality, and be comprised of a free moving spirit.

Not that this second state is a final goal, it cannot be. As a society in constant flux and in continuous contact with other regions – either for reasons of heart, trade, or commerce – we will have to take a step above this A^2 position to attain a third state, one of a community of spirit with regions and centers possessing similar customs, histories, languages, religions, myths, concerns. This new commerce of cultural histories is what pluricultural countries will strive to attain.

One may ask, "What will be the use of countries in a world composed of highly structured, self-sufficient centers?" Centers in themselves are not governments; at most, these centers can have functions similar to our present day city halls. In the same way, as no city is complete in itself, so shall no center of tomorrow be complete. The center will be a manageable culture unity in need of other centers – the same way say churches, synagogues, and mosques are self-sufficient unities in themselves, yet in evident contact with other churches, synagogues, and mosques, as well as other non-affiliated institutions. This commerce between non-affiliated centers will constitute the pluricultural federation we call the country.

To recapitulate, we believe that denationalization will give rise to regions that will not be like regions of the past; these regions will be of a higher level (what was A will become A^2). And change will not stop there, for what was B will turn to B^2.

What was the nation will become the pluricultural country.

What was A^2 separated from B^2 will become a federation of pluricultural centers ($A^3 + B^3$).

10

Ethnicity is not going to die.

The Shackles of Language

At times I feel I live in a police state. Instead of protecting citizens the police infringe on the comforts of ordinary citizens on a daily basis. Parking tickets, the paltriest of civil interference, have replaced serious investigation of organized and family crime. Comparable is the role of the language police. They discourage community celebration. Language police can be found in every country; their goal is to intrude into the freedom of laughter and to interrupt the hypnotism of participation.

In a federation of Italic peoples, it would be imperative that a police state not become the norm. The job of those working on the Italic confederation will have to travel through a network of difference; they will also have to learn to revel in difference and never ostracize what seems foreign. They will have to entice people to share a common cause.

Culture does not, however, reduce itself to language; nor does language encompass all of culture. Language is the provider of the medicine we need. Language is a young person who takes taxi after taxi, delivering the goods to those who want a particular capsule that will elevate their well-being. Elevate, augment, but not become the essence of our well-being. A person's happiness is not judged by his ability to understand Italian.

I can be a happy man without ever speaking a word of Italian. Language is a pleasurable wine that brings together people of different cultural backgrounds.

Language should be free. There can be no price tag attached to language. Language should not be exclusionary. What use is a language that places barriers preventing people from attending the gathering? Language should entice me to adopt it as a writing tool. Only language transmittable in its written form ever crosses the quagmires of time and space.

If the knowledge of a particular language is forced upon people, there will surely result a prosperous black market doing the exact opposite of what the language police wants. Spending Saturday at school learning Italian helped many boys and girls to grow wings at their ankles: no one wants to be punished for not knowing a language that his parents speak. We want to speak whatever language our friends speak.

How many times can one be accused of speaking Italian improperly? I am not a criminal for not discoursing in the language of my ancestors. Speaking the language of my grandparents is a privilege, not a penitence. A privilege similar to stumbling upon a love letter scribbled in a foreign language by a man and woman who happened to be my great grandparents. Sensations at once pleasurable and disquieting: I'm glad to happen on a secret, though it is a secret written in a code I can't decipher.

Language should provide titillation and be alluring, at times colored by a tinge of envy: we want what we can't have, and to have it we'll walk out of our way to get whatever it is that we want. Language can turn into a mechanic's dirty rag at the bottom of a oily barrel when it no longer arouses our senses. What is the fundamental appeal of a certain idiom?

In Italy, the Italian language imposed itself onto the citizens of Italy after the 1970s, thanks to state-owned TV stations. The Italian language is often what Italian TV is to the world: an anachronistic outfit that isn't exciting. Why? Because Italian is geographically delimited, sensuously discriminating, and overtly avaricious.

Often I have heard people mutter: "I am not the cousin run away from the cradle. It's those people on the TV screen who got away. It is *they* who converse in a strange language."

By some twist of fate, the people living in Italy seem to live in the past, they are fixed in a time that is not the time of Italians living outside Italy. "Why should I then learn a language belonging to 'dinosaurs?' I want to speak the language spoken by my very-much living friends."

Until the language police in Italy understands this polarity of point of view, it will never be able to seduce distant relatives into speaking Italian. "It is not the outsider but the insider who appears as an alien. It is not I who am stupid for not speaking Italian, it is you who are foolish for persisting in believing that Italian will pull you out of the iceberg you are stuck in."

Such is the mind-set of second- and third-generation Italians living abroad, yet, paradoxically, these men and women hold the key to the survival of a dying language. The principle obstacle is learning how to kindle in people from other Italic centers of the world the love of an unimportant language. "Why should I speak a language that is of no immediate interest to me?"

In Canada, where I was born, bilingualism and biculturalism have done nothing to awaken in many the need to learn the language of the Other. "If, as an anglophone, French does not interest me, why should I even waste my time in learning it?"

If a language is to inspire me, it must offer me that something special that I crave for. Whatever this thing is, it will rise from within my immediate world. Somehow the "language of the street" spread out into "the language of the mind." We cannot count on the heart alone to act as a bridge between what might have been an ancestral necessity to what is an acquired taste. To promote a foreign language one has to make it intellectually attractive.

We cannot count on Italy anymore to heighten interest in its own particular brand of artifact, past or present. "If I don't care for Dante or Lucio Dalla, then where must I turn to?" Home; that is, to my immediate center of cultural activity. Italian is not some jacket I drop over my shoulders; it must spring out of the language I speak on a daily basis: French and English.

The fact that Italy has exported more goods than it has imported has not helped it in the promotion of the Italian language, neither with people of Italian heritage, nor with people from different cultures. All exports are accompanied by an exchange of favors. What is there in the Italian language that I need? Something out there in Italy's complex extremities, though it may tickle my curiosity, was not appealing enough for many Italians living abroad. We consider ourselves Italians, but we do not speak the language. What I call the Italic reality is not a linguistic phenomenon. Nondefinable, yet palpable; recognizable, yet foreign. Whatever comprises our *Italicity* is very much a presence that goes beyond the knowledge of the Italian language.

If the Italian language is to be influential, it will have to be used to translate our foreign realities. It will have to become the receiver of new subjects. We have to translate the works of artists of both Italian and foreign extraction as well as to publicize these works in the Italian language. Italy and any other Italic centers will have to open their doors to the massive influx of exotic works. By translating and promoting the works of writers and artists of Italian background an impact will be created on artists who will want to know what it is that is being said in their name in another language.

By freeing Italian of the shackles tying it legally to a single territory, different performances of that language will be encouraged. As long as people identify Italian with Italy alone, the Italian language does not stand a chance of becoming a global language. A language attains universal status when people from every part of the world speak it on a daily basis.

Italy will also have to let go of the control it has on the ISBN (International Standard Book Number) identifying and binding the Italian language to books made in Italy. The number 88 at the back of every book published in Italy determines it as an Italian language book. Contrary to English and French, whose ISBNs are universal – that is, their numbers are not bound to geography – Italy's ISBN prefix 88 is firmly lodged in the peninsula. As long as it is, no other book written in Italian and published abroad will find its way inside the computers of Italian-language bookstores. Without the use of the 88, no book written in Italian will be recognized as an Italian-language book. Publishing an Italian-language book with a prefix such as 0 and 1 will identify it as an English-language book with an Italian title only.

May the reader forgive me for this aside into professional publishing jargon, but this is the sort of policing that is counterproductive to the universalization of the Italian language. Italy must give publishers outside Italy the permission to publish and promote Italian-language books with the proper tools. What this refusal to open up the book number has done is to effect a silencing of foreign influence on the Italian language.

The Italian language is larger than what is heard, in all its intonations and guises, in Italy. Nevertheless, unlike English, French, Spanish, and Portuguese, Italian has never had stylistic pressure from abroad to undermine the rules and regulations established by the language police in Italy.

Any sort of comparison is undermined by Italy's refusal to acknowledge the existence of the practice of "broken" Italian abroad. The French know that people in America speak and write their language differently, and it is this difference that makes French a viable artistic language for people in, say, Quebec. No such phenomenon exists with Italian. If Italian is to become vibrant it must be practiced widely, and in as many different ways as possible. American writers have totally appropriated the language of the British, and modified it forever. The British must now take American expressions into consideration when expressing themselves in English.

Translation and original linguistic styles produced abroad will help Italians find some sort of cultural solace in the near future. As long as Italy relies on export alone, its language is doomed to extinction. Italy has to expel its centripetal force and become part of the larger Italic federation. There simply does not exist enough magnetism in linguistic Italy for the language to survive globally; Italian needs foreign input to blossom worldwide.

We Could Have Been Contenders

Et si j'avais raté ma vie.
[What if I were a failure?]
Patrick Straram,
Quatre quatuors en trains qu'amour advienne

"I could have been a contender."

Marlon Brando, in the role of Terry Malloy, gives the following moving monologue near the end of Elia Kazan's 1954 masterpiece, *On the Waterfront:*

> It wasn't him, Charley. It was you. Remember that night in the Garden, when you came down to my dressing room, you said: "Kid, this ain't your night. We're going for the price on Wilson." You remember that. "This ain't your night." My night? I could have taken Wilson apart. So what happens? He gets the title shot outdoors in the ballpark. And what do I get? A one-way ticket to Palookaville. You was my brother, Charley. You should have looked out for me a little bit. You should have taken care of me, so I didn't have to take dives for short-end money. You don't understand. I could have had class. I could have been a contender. I could have been somebody, instead of a bum, which is what I am. Let's face it. It was you, Charley.

In 1980, Robert De Niro repeats this monologue in the role of the bloated and destitute Jake La Motta; it is in the last scene of Martin Scorsese's *Raging Bull.*

I found out about *On the Waterfront* by viewing *Raging Bull*. I stress this point, for it is proof that the fastest and best way to learn about the classics is by teaching contemporary works of art. The classics never lead to contemporary works, because a work of the past leads to various points in the future; whereas the contemporary work will inevitably lead us back to a precise moment in the past. Jake La Motta led me back to Terry Malloy, but Terry had no idea Jake would one day be given birth to.

Malloy is godlike in *Waterfront*. La Motta is no god, even though we sense that an unmitigated transformation is about to occur in the protagonist. "Redemption" might be the word Scorsese had in mind when he shot that final scene. De Niro's performance of an aging La Motta is as close to an epiphany as it can possibly get. The emotional charge of this moment follows a scene that shows Jake La Motta begging his brother for peace. The large crack separating the brothers seems unbridgeable. And it probably is.

★

Brothers. The story of Terry and Charley Malloy and the story of Jake and Joey La Motta are remakes of a biblical episode: the story of two brothers, Cain and Abel.

In the biblical narrative, Cain brings a fruit-offering from his land to the Lord, while Abel brings the best firstling of his flock. The Lord prefers Abel's animal offering, which makes Cain jealous, and he kills his brother. The Lord asks: "Where is your brother Abel?" Cain answers: "I don't know. Am I my brother's keeper?" The

Lord says: "What have you done? The voice of your brother's blood cries out to me from the soil." However, the Lord is not a mean god, and though he banishes Cain, he will be protected by a mark on his forehead. A nomad, Cain will marry, become a father, and the founder of a city which he'll name after his son Enoch (Genesis 4:3-17). Is it possible or even proper to compare the problem of ethnic culture to this prototype narrative of two brothers? Maybe not. Yet there is a connection. Who is asked to take a fall?

As a younger man, I sided with Abel. The victim of his murderous brother, Abel puts God on his side. As I grew older, I realized an important lesson here, which is never to take sides when it comes to family matters. Abel is no better off than Cain: both are loved by the Lord. Nor can we believe that one man's life more than the other's will lead us to paradise.

Both will die, and both will go to heaven, if heaven exists. Cain and Abel are servants of the Lord.

★

Servire. To serve. The origins of this word are in the Latin word *servire*, which means to be a slave, to live in servitude, which leads us to the Italian *servire* and the Spanish *servir:* meaning, among other things, "to be dependent on . . ." By the year 880, the word *servire* came to be associated with another idea: "to serve the devil." It was only much later, by 1050, that it began to be used in conjunction with God, as in "to serve God."

★

In the case of some poets – and I use the term here in the Aristotlean sense of the word, meaning "creators" or "artists" – the sum of their works strikes us with a powerful splendor that often is not found in their details.

Other poets excel in the detail: a singular work, or a group of works, sparkles with genius, while the sum of the individual pieces taken as a whole might leave us indifferent.

My preference is for the first kind of poet who produces a body of works that ultimately forms an entity at once intangible and overpowering. Individual pieces may not be superior, yet taken as a whole the poet's work has scope and vision.

Our critics give medals to details, instead of the total work. It's easier.

★

Winners. We live in a society that rewards success – though success is difficult to categorize. No matter, one thing is sure: someone is victorious at the end of the game.

I agree with Jean-Luc Godard who says, in *Éloge à l'amour,* a truly rare masterpiece of this era, that anyone who makes more than 4000 Francs a month has become the slave to the employer.

Success is a maker of slaves. Whether the slave is Charley more than Terry, Joey more than Jake, Cain more than Abel, I cannot say.

Does it truly make a difference?

Success comes with a price tag. You must sign your soul away. Much like Faust.

★

Not that success, as a positive experience, is bad *per se;* what is negative about success is that it seems to be a deliberate pact between two parties. On the one hand, there is a winner; on the other, a loser.

Charley and Joey both tell their brothers to willingly take a fall, that there is more profit in losing than winning. Cain's wealth comes not from losing but from killing. Which is in a sense losing. By ridding himself of Abel, he embraces an existence that his brother will never cherish. To use religious terms, it is not "good" that leads to profit but "evil."

Yet this signing of a pact with the devil is not easy. The chance for success is offered only once in a lifetime: if you don't grab it when it appears, you might as well resign yourself to being a hard but insignificant worker, hammering away in a dark shed of your life. You might turn out to be a talented blacksmith but you'll never become an internationally renowned sculptor.

The idea here is that either one becomes a slave to success or one doesn't: success is the quest, not a process.

★

The extent of success is often measured by the amount of money attached to the envelope. More legitimate than fame, financial success inevitably involves norms, rules of conduct, and zealousness. Social and cultural actions must "qualify" to be acceptable.

There was a time when we would select winners; today we *deselect* the losers. This procedure is not so much the acknowledgment of quality as the designation of what is acceptable and what is not.

Acceptability may have little to do with greatness or valor. The fact that Charley and Joey side with outlaws does not make them any less violent than Terry and Jake who improvise their own karma. No one is chosen, and this is what makes for great tragedy. To be chosen can only lead to doom. How do we qualify normalcy, poverty, marginality?

There was a time, before the seventeenth century, when the word *success* was void of moral implication; that is, its denomination did not carry adjectives that quantified the outcome. Success was the end result of a process, whether the outcome was good or bad. This idea of the natural progression of action has been totally nullified; what we underline today is only the "military" final inning that must always be victorious.

Rewards and kudos are ludicrously lavish. Call it competition, democracy, capitalism; what is promised in the end is a check mate.

But culture is not a question of winning or losing; nor can there ever be an end-game in art. As Pasquale Verdicchio says, culture is always a question of adding and subtracting. The fireworks blowing in the sky are the celebration of vexilla (flags).

★

Culture is political: this is never more evident than in time of war. "You are either with us or against us," politicians repeat.

We would be terribly naive, indeed, not to see the significance of receiving large sums of money from the elites who invest in art so as to make sure that nothing changes.

For the sake of argument, even if it were true that culture were a game of win and lose, how is it possible not to notice that the dice are loaded? The die was cast before the games were announced.

The winners are decided at the very moment the game comes into being. The list of finalists is angel dust blown into the eyes of wallflowers.

Just as the president of a country can ask his nation's film industry to produce movies to promote war, so too do the chosen few recompense those who protect the treasures of their tradition; that is, the biases of a society.

In days gone by, people in power used nepotism to promote their watermarks and emblems; today, such devices are deemed vulgar. Family members are no longer required to protect the family business. Often, the thirst for success produces virile contenders. Yet only those who serve can play. The rest become outcasts. If culture means generosity, success is the destroyer of culture.

★

When was the last time we were surprised by a winner of a major prize? You would think, with all the awards available, that there would be more contenders and winners; this is not the case.

The proliferation of awards (those little gold star stickers your teacher gives you for being the top student in your grade) does not signify that your homework is better than that of your classmates'. More often than not it is not; nevertheless, the fact that you are honored minimizes the existence of your competitors.

Awards and the success that these awards bestow on artists is a method of eradicating competition, difference, and the presence of other works of art. More now than ever, if you do not win, you do not exist.

This crazy demand for awards and social recognition surely reveals something profound and lacking in our cultures. Godard warns that people without history are now able to purchase the history of other peoples.

This scarcity of history might be responsible for the profusion of remakes and copies that are being produced everywhere and in every domain in North America. The generalization is great; the exception, the oddball. The generalization here being paradoxically the detail and not the totality. It is more convenient to rapidly reward and just as rapidly discard a piece of work that the general public recognizes than to discard a totality of works that a single poet creates. In the first case you pulp the single book; in the other you actually murder the person.

Never has the saying, "You've seen one, you've seen them all," been more meaningful. Sameness is destroying our cultures in North America.

Instead of telling himself, "Well, if XYZ won an award for a novel on immigrants, then I'll write one on inner-city life," the writer grabs on to the bandwagon and reproduces the style and content of the champion.

Whenever a copy is made quality suffers, and culture falls and breaks a limb.

A valid way to remedy this dearth of difference is to rid success of its laudatory connotations and make it the neutral concept it once was.

True success is not about winning, but about being.

★

The punch. I love Jean-Luc Godard, François Truffaut, Robert Bresson, and John Cassavetes, these are poets who belong to a select group of great filmmakers who have produced fantastic works as a whole. Yet if I had to choose my favorite single film, *Raging Bull* would be the one I'd choose, even though Scorsese is not one of my favorite filmmakers.

The black and white film stock, the violence of the acting, the animal sexuality between Jake and Vickie, the love and hate relationship between Jake and Joey, the ambitions and the final breakdown of this one man, the Italicness of the entire project: absolutely every aspect about this work disturbs me and makes me so fidgety that my own personal emotions and beliefs are shattered.

Every punch La Motta delivers to an opponent is a

punch I receive right in the face. I bleed and hurt, but I jump back on my feet and run right up to Jake and take one more punch. Good works of art hit me in the face and give me a black eye. These are not works with much financial success.

Robert Bresson died without ever amassing the necessary funds to make his dream film, *Genesis*. There are writers today who receive more money than they merit, and certainly enough money to enable more deserving artists to complete their projects. I quiver whenever I think that one of Canada's greatest writers, Patrick Straram le bison ravi, lies buried in a pauper's grave. Prizes are given to works that never rock the boat.

★

The fire. The fire is lost. Whatever blind force that led me here – emotionally, not geographically, geography is a game bored men and women play when they get too ambitious – is at its lowest point.

It was unquestionably not ambition, absence of friendship, nor the prospect of monetary gain that pushed me to move to this part of the country.

Whatever propelled me to Toronto was more like a sudden clogging of my gears, for lack of a better image.

No, I don't believe in fate, nor karma. Consciousness, yes.

A strange, yet voluntary mixing of interests congealed in me and formed into a fresh idea; it all burst forth as an unmistakable opportunity to experience life in a brand new way.

This idea to leave my hometown did not appear on the stage of my mind like a shining star, nor as a sinking stone. Some people would call it an auspicious aligning of the stars and planets. Perhaps. Or just real life.

I always wanted to leave Quebec, and this was the time to do so. I told myself, "It's now or never. And I choose *now.*"

Whatever *I* is, I found myself standing somewhere, consciously aware that one life was coming to an end and another was about to surge out of my own body. Whatever, wherever it was, I knew I had to choose coming here, to this new life, leaving behind a life that was very good to me – an extremely intense and active life.

Still I came here, unaware of the price I would have to pay. Before I unpacked my bags, I was told I had to unlearn whatever I had learned in my previous life. This was something I could not do. I refused to unlearn the lessons I was taught.

★

I chose the present tense with an intensity of being that I have only rarely ever experienced. I said *yes* to this intensity, and I said *yes* to the moving away, yet it was not truly a moving away, because it was, after all, the same country. Well, I naively believed back then that we lived in one country, *mare iusque ad mare.* But Canada is not the country we were taught about in school.

Whoever I *am* will always be there, that is here, inside of me, making me the person I am, regardless of the place I'm in, with one small difference, and that is that I am going to be *me* elsewhere.

I had nothing to lose. Not being a winner, I had to continue working and, to paraphrase Terry Malloy, I wanted to be a contender, not for the sake of winning – for I would never win in a game I did not play, or even if I did play I could not possibly win since I'm not a copycat – but because I did not think like the herd.

I wanted to be a contender, but let's face it, I am just a bum.

Being at the margins, we walk, frazzled, on the edge of the highway, move slowly, for we are not sprinters, we are long distance runners who believe in the saying: *"Chi va piano va lontano"* ("He who walks slowly goes a long way").

We carry on our shoulders the success from one part of the country to another. But it's useless.

What is more disturbing is that even when we win not a word is mentioned anywhere, so that the winning and the award are reduced to bland expression of regional fraternity.

If success does not happen, it is not due to our lack of initiative.

We are stripped naked at customs and are told to walk the white line, as though we were inebriated or stoned. At times, the guards simply say that we have lost our minds. They lock us in a cage, throwing at our feet their crumbs and dirty water. Because we are survivors, we make do. Still our family disowns us, our friends no longer understand; failure is a poet's worst enemy.

★

Je déparle. I am over-speaking, I am un-speaking, I have lost my voice, and no one hears me.

Success usually means glittering light-bulbs that one throws away as soon as they burn out. To be able to survive, as a bum, I have to first free myself, as best as I can, from the opium of one day attaining paradise.

Jake La Motta in a tuxedo, in his dressing room, cigar in mouth, shadow boxing, mutters: "It wasn't him. It was you, Charley." Yes, it is our brothers and sisters, and no one else, who pushed us into this dungeon and threw away the key.

★

It does not matter how good a poet is, if he or she does not fit the mold set up by the literary war lords of the nation who hand out the prizes, awards, and gold stars, it is no use trying. It all amounts to dust.

★

The Nation. Our cultures have become so nationalistically centered that it has become impossible to find a hint of true difference on the bookshelves in urban and rural bookstores. Of course, there are plenty of samples of slippage and cracking in the sameness, but the products are all from the same mold.

No matter where we go we keep on tripping on the usual stacks of homogeneously successful works that we have been convinced into believing are great.

To emit even a shadow of doubt makes us liable for

treason. There's no doubt, it's war-time. Every close-minded critic in the world is there to remind us that *these* books are the real works of art, that *these* are the books that connect us to our glorious past, that *these* are the films that we must protect for future generations.

History is no longer public domain, it has been copyrighted. Who are we to think otherwise?

Gaston Miron would call the writer and the publisher *un travailleur culturel* (a cultural craftsman), a person working for the betterment of his culture. How many poets today would qualify?

★

The telephone does not ring as often in our offices. There was a time when it was an honor not to answer the phone, just to be able to catch our breath and feel our heartbeat. All we do now is listen. When it's happy, we don't hear the beat at all; when it's sad, it palpitates at such a speed that at times we panic and rush to the emergency ward. Something has changed.

I have changed. And it is for the better, for I did not sign my life away to the devil. Not for a cause, not for literature, not for politics.

When writers who should be saying *thank you* start sending handwritten notes calling you a "stupid self-publishing moron, I hate Guernica books, especially yours" you know it's time to open a bottle of scotch and sit in front of your bay window and think of something else.

I embrace my new position with the same fervor as I took on the Quebecois love of sense of being and Italian refined prescience. I have still not given a name to this new passion, but it surely will never be assimilation. I am tempted here to qualify, quantify, nullify the process of assimilation, but I will not. To speak of such an idea would mean that I am willing to accept the fact that the assimilation process has already begun.

It has not. At least not in myself.

But I see assimilation now like never before. I did not see it Budapest, Hungary; I did not see it in Frankfurt, Germany. I did not see it in Paris, France, I did not see it in London, England. But I see it now everywhere. Assimilation has received another name: success. And those who do not believe in this assimilation are called reactionaries.

If what I see around me is success, then I am a failure.

★

There are two possibilities. Either the process of assimilation has begun, or else the children of immigrants are more clever than we give them credit for. I have decided to watch what I say. Maybe because I am scared, scared for my family, scared for myself, scared because I know that whatever I say or write today could tomorrow be thrown back in my face in a court of law.

I am scared also because I no longer believe in freedom of speech. I can scream as loud as I want, but if there isn't anybody out there to scream to, or if I am screaming in a sound-proof room, speech *non serve a niente.* Speech is good for nothing.

Sure, I can rejoice and step back and kiss myself, pat

myself on the shoulder, and say it'll be better tomorrow, people will read you when you're dead and gone, but I now know better.

I had my chance to be a success story. I did not take it. Maybe I could have used my success to pass on the message. I know, though, it is almost impossible for success to allow you to speak words other than those that people expect from you. Not that this is bad in itself, "Hey, why fix it if it ain't broken?" but it's clearly a question of bravery: who will spill the beans if the consequence is losing your job?

Poets produce only one kind of poem and it is the poem that he or she will write and rewrite for the rest of their lives. Every poem, every detail of a poem will always resemble the detail of another poem created by that same poet. This and that tiny parameter might vary in its shape or color but in the end young Picasso is no different than old Picasso, the erotic Picasso no different than the religious Picasso. It is this confining aspect of creativity that most fascinates me. Like Bresson would say: As an artist you are most free when you are in a prison you created for yourself.

I never enjoyed *prêt-à-porter,* nor do I see any value or merit in copies. We live in a world of copies and remakes, and it is dangerous for anyone to tread outside these clearly defined perimeters of decorum. Like in a fascist regime.

When I grew up, scholars always would warn me not to use the word *fascism* lightly, because for a regime to be fascist it had to meet a certain set of fixed criteria. And so I became extremely cautious and never used that word in a context other than the one predetermined by the meaning of the term *fascist*.

I know nothing of political science, I never took a course with a person who was a scholar in political analysis. What I know of politics is through the life I live and the information I gather by reading books by authors I respect. There are many fine political writers today. And there are terrible ones. I have discovered that a childhood friend of mine was right all along: "The Right Wing has its own brand of great thinkers." Good writing does not mean that the content is good.

Both world wars legitimized nationalist ideology. Whatever was improper about the old nationalist ideology has been uprooted, and what was good sanitized. They call it globalization now, but the names and faces of those in power have not changed.

Adolf Hitler is laughing in his grave. You can almost hear some leaders thinking out loud, as they smoke the cigars they've banned everywhere: "Extermination of populations is bad, but if we must exterminate, let's keep the numbers low."

I am appalled to see and hear how fierce the love of war has become in baby-boomers who were supposedly peaceful and so much in love with our planet and humankind. Imagine what our society would do to a writer like Boris Vian, if today he were to write a song titled "Le déserteur" *(The Deserter)*. Where has literary resistance gone to?

Murder as Spectacle

September 11
all my tv's
on the same channel

Marco Fraticelli

A friend phones from Montreal. It is about nine o'clock in the morning. I tell her I have no time to chat, there are files waiting for me on my desk. She whispers in a distressed tone:

"They've attacked the U.S.A."

I turn on the TV to CNN, surely they will be covering anything that is happening in the U.S.A.

A Boeing 767 has crashed into the North Tower of the World Trade Center. The images are taken from a camera positioned on an adjacent high-rise. The images are non-stop; we see the doors of hell opening up right in front of us. Despite the realism of these images, I refuse to take as truth what is being aired. I have not completely digested the horror of what is being shown when a second Boeing 767 rams into the South Tower of the World Trade Center.

It is 9:03 a.m. The eyes of the world are fixed to TV screens. We are all witnesses to this weird, incredible atrocity.

Obviously, this is some sick joke an arrogant film producer is sharing with us, the kind of insolent show Orson Welles launched in 1938 on radio – his *War of the Worlds*. What else can it be? How can a country as powerful as the U.S.A., with the most awesome military arsenal in the world, be allowing a catastrophe of such magnitude on its territory? Which sleeping soldiers forgot to press the red button for the antimissile attack?

For decades the Americans have been assuring us that they possess the necessary war machine to prevent this sort of disaster from happening.

The TV images are not changing. The Boeing keeps crashing into the South Tower on the ninetieth floor.

Suddenly, I feel sick. I hang up. I swallow a couple of pain-killers and drink half a bottle of spring water. The room starts to spin, everything becomes blurry. Words lose their meaning. *Love, peace, security* are being emptied of their semantic significance. The TV commentators are sweating. Is that a drop of sweat or a tear?

Whatever adjective they come up with to describe what we are witnessing seems like a wordplay. The drama unfolding over their shoulders is putting the safety of the planet into jeopardy.

Before they can even speculate on the reason for this massacre, we know that there will be massive retaliation.

Both towers crumble into the heart of our screams and tears.

I am mesmerized by the images on the TV screen and notice the shadow of my friend's house situated near the disaster area. More than just symbols, these buildings were the workplace of people I know.

I probably know victims of this atrocity in one way or another. My parents in Rivière-des-Prairies, in Montreal, are but a few miles away from New York. I phone my mother.

They have not heard the news. My mother asks what madman is behind such abomination.

"War is here," she says.

The subtle labels politicians use to classify acts of this nature become fearfully fuzzy. I collapse into a chair. I am no longer an innocent spectator. I am both a friend and an enemy, for I have so often acted like a traitor.

How many times have I imagined the collapse of this capitalist regime that destroys as much as it builds? I am in part guilty for what is happening on TV: I am an instigator of this calamity.

What divides truth and lie disintegrates. Imagination, even at its wildest configuration, begins to squint. This is the death of fiction, the death of realism. Our concepts and ideologies are more fragile than we could have imagined. Ideas are as delicate as human beings. What do I know? I am not willing to analyze an event as horrifying as this one. Any attempt at analysis would be an insult to human dignity, especially to the men and women who are falling like melting metal.

The phone rings and rings again.

A friend says, "They had it coming."

No one has death in this way coming to them. Neither the killer, nor the one who is killed.

When I was at university at Loyola, I took a course on media given by Montreal writer John Buell. He taught us that television was at the height of its strength when it caught action live.

TV at its best was a hockey game: Canada versus

ANTONIO D'ALFONSO

Russia. At its worst, the assassination of the Kennedy brothers or Lee Harvey Oswald.

This is when the camera lets go of its role as passive spectator and becomes the living witness of history in the making. TV in all its splendor.

The horror rises as quickly as our awareness of becoming victims to its witness.

No wonder people wanted to broadcast Timothy McVeigh's execution. The world wanted to see the U.S. worst terrorist die just as he had killed hundreds of men and women who happened to have been in a federal building in Oklahoma City on a fateful day.

TV loves yelling at us: "What is more exciting: seeing a person live or die? What gives more pleasure?"

What TV demands from its greedy spectators is that we weep at the same time the enemy is wincing with joy.

The ambiguity of death.

Later.

We are told that a certain man from California by the name of John Walker has been arrested. He is accused of fighting in the Islamic *jihad* on the side of the Taliban. Some people say that he applauded the destruction of the twin towers. Without missing a beat, the president of the U.S.A. has sentenced this man to death for treason.

But here's the snag. By constitutional law, convicting someone of treason requires two witnesses to the treasonous act. Where do we find these witnesses? TV was not there.

The New York tragedy has forever divided the

American people into two clans: the patriots and the traitors.

No one is laughing now. No one is applauding. We know we are not supposed to laugh at murder. To inflict a fatal blow on the enemy is an assassination. Whether the assassin is motivated by a revolutionary ideal or commissioned by some mob lord, the consequences are the same.

Living is a right. Killing is an outrage. (The call to arms could be viewed as a contract criminal organizations hand out to mercenaries.) No matter where you stand on the political spectrum, the attack of 11 September 2001 is the most calamitous of assassinations ever televised. There have been other crimes in modern times – the Nazi concentration camps, Hiroshima, Nagasaki – but none captured in real-time. To offer the horror of murder as a spectacle is to encourage ignorance. What do we learn by watching these images of murder, be it of one person or an entire community? And what is ominous is that there is no end to it in sight. We, the thrill-seekers, know that after seeing one group of religious fanatics commit suicide on TV there is another spectacle not far behind.

The world no longer belongs to us. Massacres are followed by more massacres. The latest massacre of innocent working men and women makes it harder and harder to shut the book of human imbecility.

"He who is not with us is against us." Why are the heads of our Western nations screaming at us?

Pacificism has once again become synonymous with stupidity. A pacificist is someone who lacks common sense. A journalist writes: "How dare you criticize our democratic institutions?"

I for one did not want to see what I saw on that sinister day on TV.

I who no longer pray am praying for the gods to stay up in heaven. That is all we need now: for divinities to come down and turn our earthly paradise into hell.

A kilogram of human flesh is worth more than a gram of uranium.

> I am nothing . . .
> I am a failure . . .
> Yet I carry within me all the dreams of the world.
>
> Fernando Pessoa,
> *The Poems of Alvaro de Campos*

Sources

I would like thank the Ontario Arts Council (the Writers' Reserve program) for its financial support and encouragement. My gratitude goes to Elana Wolff for her meticulous editing and hortative whispers, and Elisabeth Pouyfaucon who guided me through this revised edition. All of these texts were written for a particular occasion, I thank the friends and editors who commissioned them. These texts have been totally rewritten.

"By Way of Introduction": Toronto, 30 November 2000-29 July 2003. Thank you, Judit Molnár.

"The Red Herring": 17 March 1999. Unpublished.

"Answering Questions: Interview with Susana Molinolo": 3 July 2003, Bluewater, Georgian Bay. Published in *Surface and Symbol,* Vol. 16, No. 6, July/August 2004.

"On Publishing": Toronto, 10 May 1996. To Maria Mazziotti Gillan. Read in Paterson, N.J.

"The Future of Italic Culture": Toronto, 5-8 March1997. Published as an interview given to Alessandro Bottero in *Il Messaggero di Sant'Antonio,* Padova, Italia, maggio 1997. Translated in Bluewater, Ontario, 18 July 2003.

"Alter rem, alter valorem": written between 1-12 October 1997. Read at an Italian-American conference at SUNY, U.S.A.

"Rooting for the Opposite Team": Written on 10 March 1999. It might have been published in *Tandem.*

"Failure": Published in French in *Liberté,* Volume 44, No. 258, Number 4, November 2002. Translated in Bluewater, Ontario, on 16 July 2003. I want to thank and dedicate this piece to Paul Bélanger for having edited the original text. Read at the ABECAN conference in Belo Horizonte, Brazil, 10 November 2003: Published in *Perspectivas Transnacionais,* edited by Sandra Regina Goulart Almeida, Brazil: Belo Horizonte: Universidade Federal de Minas Gerais, 2005. Thank you, Sandra Almeida.

"Translation: A Sacrifice": Published in *La traducière,* Paris, 1984. Thank you, Jacques Rancourt.

"The Quest for Authenticity" : Recorded in Montreal, 6 October 2002. Published in French in *Exit,* No. 30, Winter, Montreal: Éditions Gaz Moutarde, 2003. Thank you, Denise Brassard.

"The Book Crisis": Written on 22 May 2002.

"Je m'accuse": Written in Toronto, 6 February 2000. Translated in Bluewater, on 12 July 2003. Published in *Tribune juive,* Volume 17, numéro 2, 2000. Thank you, Ghila Sroka.

"Talking with Students": 1-17 May 2000. Written dialogue with students from the French department at the University of Toronto.

"11.04.1985": Published in *Poetry Canada* in 1985.

"07.08.1984": Published in *Poetry Canada*. 7 August 1984.

"Nick's Pain": Published in *Painting Moments,* edited by Mary Melfi. Guernica, 1998.

"28.10.1987": Published in *Poetry Canada* in 1987.

"24.04.2002": Parts in *Poetry Canada,* 26 April 1988. The quote is by Robin Skelton, writing about *The Passions of Mr. Desire* by André Roy, translated by Daniel Sloate. Guernica, 1986.

"01.07.1997": Toronto, 1 July 97: *Toronto Star:* Rosie DiManno's "Growing up on Grace."

"16.11.1998": For *Tandem*. Thank you, Angela Baldassarre.

"25.11.1998": For Colin Vaughan.

"01.08.1996": Published in *Tandem,* 10 August 1996.

"An Italic in Paris": Written and read at the Salon du livre de Paris, 22-24 March 2002, that year dedicated to Italian literature; translated in Bluewater, 13 July 2003.

"That Hidden Resource Beneath the Ashes": Translated by Emanuele Oriano and the author. Published in *Corriere canadese* and *Tandem,* 1999.

"Making Italian a Living Language": Published in *Tandem,* 12 January 2001.

"The Impracticability of Having One Major Center": Published in *Tandem,* 2001. Thank you, Antonio Maglio.

"A Conversation with Jennifer Sipos": Filmed in Toronto, April 2002.

"Virtual Ethnics": Toronto, 12-13 April 1999. Given as a lecture at the Dufferin Library. 13 April 1999. Written on a plane on my way back from a lecture tour in Germany. Thank you, Gino Chiellino (Augsburg), Franco Biondi (Hanau), Beatrice Bagola (Trier), and all the other men and women I met in Bavaria.

"Markings": Written on the plane from Augsburg to Toronto on 18 November 1992. Thank you, Gino Chiellino.

"The Shackles of Language": Commissioned by Sergio Roic, for the Italian magazine, *Dialogica* (Switzerland). Written on 22 May 2005 and revised on 6 July 2005.

"We Could Have Been Contenders": 30 November 2000-Montreal, 6 February 2002, Toronto. Read at the Columbus Center, 8 February 2002. Thank you, Elio Costa and York University.

"Murder as Spectacle": Written in French between 20 December 2001 and 22 January 2002. Published in *Le 11 Septembre des poètes du Québec.* Edited by Louis Royer. Montreal: Éditions Trait d'Union, 2002. Translated on 3-4 August 2003. Thank you, Louis Royer.

By the Same Author

La chanson du shaman à Sedna (1973)
Queror (1979)
Black Tongue (1983)
Quêtes: Textes d'auteurs italo-québécois
(with Fulvio Caccia, 1983)
Voix off: Textes de dix poètes anglophones
au Québec (1985)
The Other Shore (1986, 1988)
L'autre rivage (1987, 1999)
L'Amour panique (1988)
Avril ou L'anti-passion (1990)
Julia (1992)
Panick Love (1992)
Fabrizio's Passion (1995, 2000)
In Italics: In Defense of Ethnicity (1996)
L'apostrophe qui me scinde (1998)
Duologue: On Culture and Identity
(with Pasquale Verdicchio, 1998)
En Italiques: Réflexions sur l'ethnicité (2000, 2005)
Comment ça se passe (2001)
Getting on with Politics (2002)
Antigone (2004)
Un vendredi du mois d'août (2004)
Bruco (2005)
Un homme de trop (2005)
A Friday in August (2005)